MW00799997

Grassroots Sustainability
A Guide to Organizing a Thriving Community

Lisa Chipkin & Pam Hartwell-Herrero

Illustrations by Jen Jones & Kristin Jakob

GRASSROOTS SUSTAINABILITY
Fairfax, California

Library of Congress Control Number 2012903293
ISBN 978-1-105-57453-5 (trade pbk.)

Printed in the United States of America

Publisher Note:

This book showcases local action that can be replicated in any community with a bit of organizing, some persistence and a whole lot of good work. It is intended to be used as a guide and workbook for individuals and groups seeking to make positive change in their communities.

Certain design choices were made to facilitate group process: Lined pages promote ease of note-taking and brainstorming in the creation and development of new community organizations and local actions. The content has been kept short and to the point for quick reference and inspiration, and to allow groups to get out in the community and do the work.

We invite you to share the book's contents to facilitate your local work, but please contact us for permission should you seek to charge for it. You can find us at **www.GrassrootsSustainability.org**.

Begin - A Poem by Rumi

This is now. Now is,
all there is. Don't wait for Then;
strike the spark, light the fire.

Sit at the Beloved's table,
feast with gusto, drink your fill

then dance
the way branches
of jasmine and cypress
dance in a spring wind.

The green earth
is your cloth;
tailor your robe
with dignity and grace.

Table of Contents

Responding to Your Passion and Concern

"When I speak to high school students, I often apologize for the future we are burdening them with and tell them 'it is just like us humans to use our intelligence, creativity and resources to completely mess the world up, and, it is also just like us humans to use our intelligence, creativity and resources to find a way to fix it.'"

Pam Hartwell-Herrero, Sustainable Fairfax

You have picked up this guide for a reason– It may be your awareness of an overwhelming list of challenges we face on the planet: climate change, peak oil and other dwindling resources, drought, corporate personhood, toxin build up, species and habitat loss, social injustices, skyrocketing rates of obesity and diabetes, plastic garbage "islands" in our oceans– the list goes on and on.

Perhaps you are scared, angry or heartbroken at the damage we've done to the planet and the apathy of the masses. Or you are a parent who has just figured out that the future really is important, or a student wondering if we will ever get out of this mess. Maybe you have been active on some of these issues for years and are looking for fresh ideas. Or the Occupy movement has inspired you to stand up and help bring social and economic justice and power to your community. Or you simply feel inspired to make a difference.

Why you are reading this guide is important, but not as important as the actions you will take next to forward sustainability in your community.

People who bring about powerful change in the world often start with a simple decision to respond to something about which they feel passionate. They begin with an idea or a vision, then take small actions that progressively build into larger ones and make a meaningful impact over time. They never succumb to the idea that one person cannot make a difference. Nor do they surrender to thoughts such as, *Someone else will probably take care of that*, or, *I just don't have time to do anything about it*. They simply decide that an issue is important enough for them to give time and energy to, then roll up their sleeves and get to work.

People like this are not alone. Recent books such as Blessed Unrest by Paul Hawken, or The Sustainability Revolution by Andres Edwards chronicle a growing wave of individuals, governments, businesses, communities, schools, organizations, grassroots groups and neighborhood associations all taking part in a "Sustainability Revolution." People around the globe from all walks of life are standing up and empowering themselves to address a plethora of challenges in an effort to live more sustainably on the planet. The result is a palpable shift, as the call to action spreads like wildfire around the globe. Little by little, the collective efforts of many are beginning to move mountains.

Inspiration in Marin County, California

Just north of San Francisco, Marin County has a rich history of environmental activism that has preserved it from over-development and resulted in its "no-growth" policy. Only twenty five percent of its natural land is developed, with open space, parks, wetlands and agricultural lands comprising the remaining seventy-five percent. Its special history has created a solid foundation upon which to build, and a legacy to uphold.

In 1972, several activists and leaders of these early efforts helped to establish the Environmental Forum of Marin (EFM), a non-profit organization dedicated to preserving the quality of the environment in Marin County. Still going strong today, EFM has consistently provided environmental education and advocacy training to community members at a wildly affordable cost. From it has sprung a profusion of citizen advocates who have gone on to effect positive change of all sorts within their communities.

Over the past ten years or so, a series of sister organizations affectionately called "The Sustainables" have emerged in towns and cities across the county. Most were founded by recent EFM graduates who shared a sense of urgency about the social, economic, and environmental crises we face on our planet, as well as a belief that they could help shape a more sustainable world by starting with local action in their back yards. In most cases, they had little to no experience running community organizations, making public policy, advocating for cultural and regulatory change, or teaching. But with their passion and determination guiding them, they went to work to actively build sustainability into the fabric of their communities. And they have had quite a lot of success.

This guide is based on their efforts. It shares their hard won lessons, successes, failures and inspiration, along with some basic tools and tips for individuals and groups wanting to get started in their own communities. It is by no means an exhaustive resource, but is intended to empower, provide guidance, and save time and energy as you join your local efforts to the collective efforts slowly but surely moving mountains around the world.

"It's been an astonishing revelation to me to see how powerful a small group of people can be, particularly locally, where you have the most power: Your small group of people can urge the City Council to do things. It's just amazing, and it makes sense to do it because it affects your own life more than anything else will. Getting local is the name of the game in sustainability. Even before we understood this, we knew it was easier to move the ball locally than anywhere else: The further away you get from home, the harder it is to move the ball."

~ Marie Kerpan, Sustainable Mill Valley

CHAPTER ONE

Where to Start? Giving Yourself Some Background

What Is Sustainability, Anyway?

First defined in 1987 by the United Nations designated World Commission on Environment and Development (the Brundtland Commission), sustainability is seen as "a concept, a field, and a set of growing practices."

Its definition continues to evolve as organizations, academic institutions, nations and individuals work at it. Some popular definitions include the following:

"We must join together to bring forth a sustainable global society founded on respect for nature, universal human rights, economic justice, and a culture of peace. Towards this end, it is imperative that we, the peoples of Earth, declare our responsibility to one another, to the greater community of life, and to future generations."

The Earth Charter, originally an initiative of the United Nations, which seeks to establish the metrics, values and direction needed to achieve sustainability. (www.earthcharterinaction.org)

"[Meeting] the needs of the present without compromising the ability of future generations to meet their own needs."

The Brundtland Commission

"Improving the quality of human life while living within the carrying capacity of supporting eco-systems."

International Union for Conservation of Nature (www.iucn.org), the United Nations Environmental Program (www.unep.org), and The World Wildlife Fund (www.worldwildlife.org).

"Thriving in Perpetuity."

Overheard at a Teens Turning Green Conference. (www.teensturninggreen.org)

Sustainability is commonly organized around the inextricably interdependent *three E's of sustainability*: Environment, social Equity, and Economy. When imagined as the three legs of a stool, we can easily see that if one leg is weak or broken, the stool is in danger of collapsing. Prioritizing focus on one leg often leads to the compromise and degradation of the others. Conversely, if all three are given equal value, energy and ingenuity, the result is something solid and lasting. Applying this concept to a nation or institution, a city or town, a school or a business creates the possibility for all involved to "thrive in perpetuity."

Environment

According to the World Wildlife Fund's *2004 Living Planet* report, we are currently exceeding the natural world's capacity to support and provide for us by over twenty percent, and that number continues to rise exponentially. A booming human population, an addiction to material consumption, and a long history of reckless exploitation of natural resources for economic gain have resulted in broad environmental degradation and depletion. Evidence of this includes the collapse of ocean fisheries, the loss of plant and animal species at an alarming rate, the destruction of rain forests, the disappearance of top soil, and the shortage of clean, fresh water worldwide.

Humans have long counted on nature to provide an abundance of resources and vital life support services for free. Referred to as "natural capital," some of these include food, water, natural fiber, timber, air and water purification, climate regulation and pollination.

The dwindling and/or degradation of natural capital due to short-sighted business practices and resource mining has not historically been factored into the cost of doing business. But there are now efforts being made to assign monetary value to natural capital so that its degradation and destruction, or preservation and restoration become necessarily factored in to the cost of doing business. This will create incentives for governments, businesses, manufacterers and landowners to preserve and restore natural capital and engage in less destructive, more regenerative practices, or see their bottom lines negatively affected should they continue business as usual.

Social Equity

"Social capital" is seen as the energy, skills, creativity, productivity and ingenuity of individuals in a community, business or organization. Social capital is what drives local, national and global economies. In a sustainable world, all generations, current and future, deserve equal opportunity to be make valuable contributions to their community, be valued, and achieve economic and social well-being. Here the question becomes, how can the quality of life for all be improved without negatively impacting any? Social equity means fair, just and equitable treatment of all people, regardless of gender, age, economic status, ethnicity or physical ability. It ensures all members of a community have access to healthcare, education, employment, safety and security, shelter, clean air, food and water.

Economy

A prevalent business model has been one that serves the bottom line, a 'profit first, people and planet later' model. But a sustainable model is based on a "triple bottom line," one that recognizes and values the inseparability of all three E's.

Economic vitality comes through sustainable business practices which allow businesses of all types to remain profitable enough to ensure their long-term survival while enhancing and renewing the resources they depend on: social and natural capital and the communities in which they do business.

Sustainable Community

In a sustainable community, the "triple bottom line" model becomes an inherent part of all business plans, building designs, city ordinances, policies and practices.

A necessary accompaniment to this is a shared commitment by community shareholders to seeking continual improvement of all three E's, measuring progress consistently and making appropriate adjustments as needed.

What Does Sustainability Look Like in Your Community?

While nation-states, educational institutions and global organizations have done important work defining, designing and implementing sustainability, tremendous local action is also needed to implement it. Top-down, bottom-up and side-to-side strategies are called for. This is where you come in to help spur tangible and effective change in your community.

To begin your work, take a look around your community with the three E's in mind. What is the relative state of health of each of them, or the lack thereof?

To find out, here are some ideas to get you started:

- Contact your City Council and staff to learn if there are existing ordinances governing things like green building, commercial plastic bag use, pesticide use, and greenhouse gas reduction.

- Approach environmental and social justice groups and ask where they see gaps.

- Look at the local economic climate- are businesses thriving or failing? Are community members employed locally or traveling great distances to work?

- How are local resources being used or abused?

Before diving in to attempt any quick fixes, take some time to understand the complexities that might lie beneath the surface. This awareness will allow you to collaborate more compassionately and successfully with local business leaders, government officials, public agencies, school districts, and non-profit organizations. It will also help you to be more effective and intelligent as you design, plan and execute actions that move toward long-term solutions and a community model based on a "triple bottom line."

Don't get discouraged if it seems like a Herculean task. In the words of Ed Quevedo, a revered professor of Sustainable Practices, simply "start where you are, use what you have, and do what you can.

Environmental Sustainability

There is a reason most people think of this as the most crucial area to work with. Thriving populations and economies rely on the sustaining support of a healthy natural environment.

To move this forward in your community, consider:

- Clean energy programs
- Plastic bag bans
- Halting the use of toxic pesticides through Integrated Pest Management (IPM)
- Responsible water and watershed management
- Climate Change Action Programs and greenhouse gas reduction
- Green building ordinances
- Waste handling, resource recovery and recycling
- Local, sustainable food production

Sustainable Social Equity

A sustainable and resilient community is one that is connected, where people look out for one another, help ensure people's basic needs are met and that there is general fair treatment and well-being throughout. But in many instances, we have become increasingly isolated from the people living and working in our communities.

How do you get your community involved in having the larger conversation about sustainability and working towards more and more inclusivity? Here are some areas of focus to help you think about this:

To move this forward in your community, consider:

- Affordable housing
- Environmental burdens borne by segments of the population, often minorities
- Affordable and accessible healthcare
- Access to clean air and water
- Access to recreation, green spaces and parks
- Active neighborhood groups and associations
- Emergency preparedness
- Neighborhood environmental and social quality

- The distance between jobs and residences of lower income workers and the impact on their ability to maintain quality of life and care for children
- Access to nutritious foods or the opportunity to have gardens in cities
- Education to re-skill people to grow their own food
- Direct connection between food producers and consumers
- Access to quality education, libraries and other knowledge archives
- Open, transparent, and participatory governance
- Fair and equitable treatment of all groups
- Cultural relations in which the positive aspects of different cultures are valued and protected, and in which cultural integration is supported and promoted when it is desired by individuals and groups
- Effective, fair, and equitable legal and police systems
- A healthy built environment
- Affordable, efficient transportation

Sustainable Economy

"Big Box" stores have driven a great many small and locally-owned businesses to closure or the brink of closure. Mass-produced foreign goods, often manufactured with toxic methods and materials using exploitative labor have virtually replaced unique, hand-produced goods made with local or sustainable natural resources. The wastefulness, human rights violations and degradation often associated with the production, storage, distribution, and disposal of these goods clearly contribute to our, social and economic decline.

An important goal here is to re-create a strong, resilient and diverse set of ecologically sound local systems to produce and distribute goods that are truly needed by the population without creating waste, pollution or excess. Another goal is to insure a business climate that provides people with local jobs that offer fair wages and equitable treatment.

Identifying locally-owned businesses and sustainably-made products and supporting them with your dollars again and again is a great way to build sustainability into the local economy. Tim LaSalle of the Rodale Institute states that *"not only do local businesses generate more local income, jobs, and tax receipts, but they also tend to utilize advertising, banks and services in the local community. In fact, a dollar spent at a local business turns over seven times in that community; while the same dollar spent at a box store or chain only turns over 2.5 times."*

Encourage community members to consider whether they are supporting or degrading their local economy and the planet with each dollar they spend.

To move this forward in your community, consider:

- Localization of goods and services
- Developing relationships with the people who produce food and offer services locally
- Access to safe employment opportunities
- Fair wages that provide for a decent standard of living
- Local job development
- Fair practices and treatment in the workplace
- Engaging with the Chamber of Commerce
- Working with local government to apply for CittaSlow (www.cittaslowusa. org) or The Business Alliance for Local Living Economies (BALLE- www. livingeconomies.org)
- Creating local currency vouchers, coupons or tokens

Meeting the Players Involved

As you consider your community through the lens of sustainability, you will likely find there are many individuals and local organizations already working on elements of sustainability. Your initial encounters with them will determine whether they become your allies or classify you as a threat or nuisance to be ignored.

As you meet people, be respectful of their time and clear about your desire to learn how you can fit in or support further progress. Consider that they have already done a great deal of work perhaps in the face of some adversity. Above all, avoid complaining that there is not enough being done. You might offer them a cup of coffee or lunch to facilitate conversation and friendship. Meet on their turf. Ask about the passion or motivation they feel for doing the work they do, and listen for what will likely be very telling answers. Take careful notes during this inquiry and record:

- Organization names and missions
- Service area
- Important contact people
- Phone numbers and email addresses
- Personal passions and pet projects
- Connections that link people or organizations to one another.

Cataloguing this information will serve you down the road, providing a quick reference each time you seek community partners for collaboration or support.

Common Threads: Where To Start? ~ Giving Yourself Some Background

- *Let Passion, Interest and Concern Guide You.* Don't worry about a lack of experience, just begin!
- *Be Curious.* Look around your town or city at what sustainability-related work is or is not happening.
- *Identify Needs.* See where there are holes or gaps you could help fill in.
- *Find Players and Partners.* Identify who is already at work on your issue or related issues. Begin to make connections.

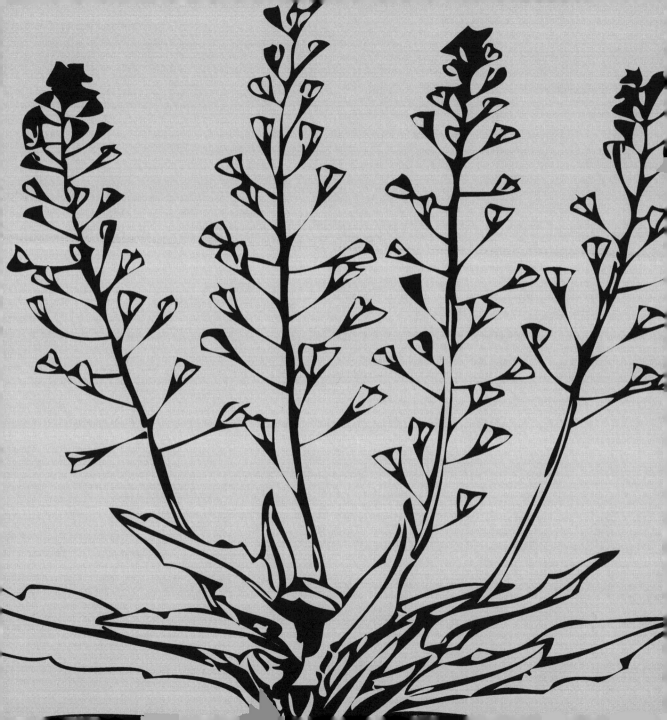

CHAPTER TWO

Create Your Team! Organizing for Long-Term Success

"You have to find the core group of very passionate people who share your ideals. They may not share your expertise; in fact it's better to be very diverse in expertise. But you have to find some way to coalesce that group in whatever city or town you are in. Start with that and organize."

Anan Paterson, Sustainable Novato

Never forget that a small group of well-organized, intelligent and persistent people can accomplish great things. Gathering a team of people to explore ideas, plan, share the workload and offer each other support will make your work a lot more fun, meaningful and effective. Groups, even small ones, tend to have more influence and be taken more seriously by City Councils, government agencies and school districts than individuals, as there is power in numbers. The more people you have behind you, the easier it will be to effect change in your community.

Look around your community for like-minded people who share your passion for sustainability and a desire to work for change. Seek people with whom you think you can work well, and whose interests and talents complement yours. If in your initial explorations you discover a group already working on sustainability, you may decide it makes sense for you to join them. After all, there are limited resources of "extra" time, money and energy in every community. Working together can multiply their effect.

Whether you will be starting a new group or joining an existing one, take some time to get to know the people involved, accept that they will be perfectly imperfect, and consider sharing this guide with them when appropriate. With a thoughtful approach, your group can set itself up for success.

Getting Organized

If you will be launching a new organization, don't be afraid to take adequate time early on to make agreements about how your group will function, communicate and come to decisions. While this may delay your initial work in the community, the pay-off will be more effective and efficient work down the road.

Implosions can be common in grassroots groups that neglect this early organizing, as was the case for several of the groups featured in this guide. But these early lessons led them to re-organize in a way that would ultimately sustain them.

"[Sustainable Fairfax] started out just having fun doing as much as they possibly could to make good things happen in Fairfax. They were very active in lots of education, policy moves, and projects. But anyone could be on the board, and it is my understanding that the board meetings would last hours and had no real structure. [The organization] was entirely consensus-based so everybody in the room had to agree on a thing before it moved forward. Decisions became too hard to make, and it just got to be too much."

Pam Hartwell-Herrero, Executive Director, Sustainable Fairfax

Because your group will likely be volunteer driven, and because people have busy lives, it is important to maximize your organizational structure early on. With some strategic pre-planning, the organization's crucial social capital resources- people's time, energy and creativity- can be channeled efficiently and the work distributed in a way that is manageable for all. Too often, one or two people can end up carrying too large a load, leading to early burnout and the ultimate failure of an organization. A lack of structure can also lead to inefficient meetings and ineffective work.

I think every non-profit [or grassroots] organization has to go through these sometimes painful developmental steps

along the way. That happened for us over the last two years in developing our structure and our funding. Painful because it takes a great deal of patience, time and effort to think of all the details, put them down in writing, get consensus on initiatives, and then execute and implement them."

Marie Chan, Sustainable Novato

In Appendix C of this guide, there is are many online and print resources available to help you develop formal structure, and there are many more on the internet and beyond. You may also look at your local community for other resources such as classes, coaching or mentoring.

Core members of Sustainable Fairfax worked with a local organization to hone in on the organizational mission, vision, and structure that had been lacking in their early work. Community at Work (www. communityatwork.com) works with non-profit organizations to develop structure, group facilitation and decision-making for greater success, and helped Sustainable Fairfax to regroup stronger than ever.

Several Sustainable Novato board members took basic board management classes through the local Center for Volunteer and Non-profit Leadership of Marin (www. CVNL.org). CVNL offers classes, advisors, a library and a resource rich website.

Which Organizational Model Will Work Best For You?

"[It's been] a process of learning how to [formalize our organization's structure], at the same time as developing the credibility of our organization. We went through this kind of mushy period of 'this has to be done, who's in the front line to do it?' to becoming more functionally oriented, to getting the job done in a more efficient way and giving other people an opportunity to do their work and feel ownership and empowerment."

Kiki LaPorta, Sustainable San Rafael

Two common models for organizing are the 'issues or initiatives–based' model and the 'function-based' model:

In the issues or initiatives-based model, small groups are formed based on topics like climate change, water, food, toxics, affordable housing or green building. Each group then focuses its work in the community around their single issue.

In the function-based model, individuals take on specific roles to deal with functions such as marketing, fund-raising, special projects or educational events that address all initiatives via these roles.

There are pros and cons to both models. The issues or initiatives-based model tends to draw people who are very passionate about a particular issue. But, if this issue gets resolved, or there is extensive down time due to governmental bureaucracy or something else, these passionate volunteers can lose interest and move on to other projects outside of your group.

The function-based model defines clear roles for each member, which results in less debate about whose job is whose, and encourages collaboration amongst the roles. But the narrow focus of the roles can appear less enticing and make it sometimes challenging to find volunteers willing to take them on.

Assembling Your Leadership Team

"We were growing, and part of what we needed to do to grow was to get serious about not trying to solve every problem during the board meetings. So we instituted a sub-committee structure: governance, finance, development, with each of our strategic initiatives having a sub-committee as well."

John Schlag, Sustainable Novato

Your leadership team or board of directors consists of the Executive Board and the issues and initiative or functional committee chairs. It may also include ad hoc members who offer mentorship, expertise or advice in certain areas relevant to the work of your organization. (It is a good idea not have too many ad hoc members or the meeting can be consumed by information sharing versus planning for action.)

The board should meet regularly throughout the year, and should review its structure, expertise and commitment at least once annually to insure maximum effectiveness. This review can be built into an annual retreat which can also serve as a team-building event.

A good board will provide challenge and opportunity for all the people involved. Ideally and often naturally, your board will contain a balance of different types of personalities, expertise, passions and skill sets. You might have the 'big picture' person, the 'brainiac', the 'detail-oriented' person, the 'statistician', the 'technical expert', the 'feisty activist' and the 'grounded organizational type.' Recognizing these elements within your board and knowing how to best utilize them will be tremendously beneficial to your work.

If you have positions you want to fill, consider creating job descriptions and recruiting people to fill them. Make sure to clearly define the amount of time required so people know what kind of commitment they will be making.

Board Responsibilities:

The Executive Board consists of the following roles. The responsibilities of each role can be determined by the board and written into its by-laws, but are generally defined as follows:

President/Chair

General: Ensures the board is taking effective action and that all board members are fulfilling their responsibilities. Oversees recruitment, assignment and orientation of new board members.

Community: Represents the organization in the community and to the media (as does the Executive Director, if there is one). Works with the Executive Director to develop meeting agendas, and chairs board meetings.

Committees: Recommends what committees are needed to the board. Ensures each committee chair is fulfilling their responsibilities. Recruits new committee chairs as needed.

Work Regarding Executive Director (if applicable): Establishes committee to hire Executive Director. Leads board discussions and evaluations of Executive Director, and determines Executive Director compensation.

Vice President/Vice-Chair

Assumes responsibilities of the president/chair in his or her absence and assists the president/chair on his or her specified duties. Often chairs a major committee of the board.

Secretary/Scribe

Records or ensures the accurate recording of the actions of the board in the minutes. Signs the minutes and distributes them to all board members. Keeps track of all important board documents, including by-laws, minutes and other items, such as important correspondence.

Treasurer

General: Keeps accurate financial records for the group. Handles all deposits and disburses payments as ordered by the board.

Reports: Makes appropriate financial reports available to the board.

Finance Committee: Chairs the Finance Committee and creates agendas for its meetings.

Executive Director

General: Responsible for carrying out the strategic initiatives and policies established by the board.

Community: Represents the organization in the community and to the media.

Committees: Recruits and orients committee chairs. Oversees all committee work to ensure effectiveness.

Fundraising: Oversees fundraising efforts. Identifies funding resources, submits proposals and administers grants received. Often required to fund own position. The Executive Director is often responsible for securing the funding for his or her position.

Hiring Staff

If you are considering hiring an Executive Director or other staff, such as administrative assistant or bookkeeper, you will need to establish your group as a non-profit or find another non-profit organization to act as your fiscal sponsor. 9[For more on this, see *Chapter 7: What Will It Cost Us? Funding Your Work.*)

How To Populate Your Board or Advisory Board with Good People:

Look around locally for sustainability experts, leaders and like-minded folk. When you meet them, make a connection and acknowledge their talent and good work. Let them know what you're doing and invite them to join you. Don't be afraid to ask a busy person; busy people get things done!

"When you acknowledge people's work, their generosity of spirit and intention, and you ask them to help, they're far more willing to step up and respond in a positive way. That's been my experience, and I've been very gratified that we've brought some really good, strong people on."

Kiki LaPorta, Sustainable San Rafael

Protocols for board participation and responsibilities should be made clear up front when recruiting. Sustainable Fairfax provides the example on the following pages to communicate this to interested parties.

Example: Sustainable Fairfax's Board Structure and Organizational Model

Executive Committee: Traditional roles, with the exception of the Vice President, who also acts as Chair for the Policy Committee.

The board is populated with the Chairs of each of the following committees:

The Sustainability Center Committee: Runs and maintains the Sustainability Center, a rented house and garden in downtown Fairfax demonstrating sustainable practices and open to the community on weekends. Develops and offers informal mini-classes for community members who drop into the center. Committee members keep the center looking nice, manage retail, keep educational displays and signage updated as needed, ensure the center is staffed, weed the backyard, and do whatever needs to be done, including cleaning.

Policy Committee: Looks at the top issues or strategic initiatives for the year and has volunteers on the committee attend relevant policy related meetings in the community. Volunteers report back to the board and larger community via Sustainable Fairfax's newsletter and website, as well as create related educational displays in their center.

Occasionally, if committee members get really fired up about an issue related to policy, they produce an event for the public. In the past, such events have included a forum on "Where Will Our Trash Go?" (which addressed an unpopular landfill expansion) a city-wide plastic bag ban, and a panel on "Marin Clean Energy" (which demystified a new Joint Powers Energy Authority in the county).

Marketing and Communications Committee: Publishes e-newsletter every two weeks, sends out media alerts, press releases and community announcements for all events, and keeps website up to date and looking good.

Example: Sustainable Fairfax's Board Structure and Organizational Model *(continued)*

Volunteer Training Committee: Handles the intake of new volunteers, facilitates volunteer trainings, organizes volunteers and the staffing of the center and all events, oversees a Yahoo group for the volunteers.

Community Education Committee: Designs and coordinates all monthly community education events. (A larger committee works well so that people can take turns being lead organizer for different events.)

Project Committee: Facilitates weekly education and action called 'Green Wednesdays' at the Fairfax Farmers Market, and coordinates with other community groups who want to co-create or co-produce projects or events to ensure established protocol is followed (criteria for project is met, process for how it gets done is followed).

Development Committee: Fundraises through business and individual memberships, fundraising parties, grant writing and events.

Board Participation: Basic Board Understandings

- Your presence is required for all board meetings- your voice is necessary to sustain this organization. A 2/3 quorum is required for votes.

- We rotate facilitation duties. Take your turn and learn how to run a meeting effectively. See sample agendas for board and committee meetings to design your agenda.

- We will start on time. Arrive 15 minutes early to have a cup of tea and socialize.

- We will not go back over items that have been missed by someone because they were late.

Example: Sustainable Fairfax's Board Structure and Organizational Model *(continued)*

- If you are unable to attend, let the facilitator know ahead of time and if you are able, send someone from your committee.

- If a board member is habitually late or does not attend, the President or Executive Director will take the following steps to resolve the issue:

    -Talk to the board member in question,
    -Issue a warning,
    -Remove board member from board if the issue cannot be resolved.

- To put a big business item before the board (an issue that needs board discussion and/or a vote), send a written report to the facilitator one week before meeting so s/he can distribute it to the board for consideration prior to the meeting.

- The board works more effectively if they have a draft proposal to work with rather than an open-ended question or problem.

- We will end on time. It is the facilitator's job to end meetings on time, but everyone can help by keeping a check on themselves.

- If a board member feels they are no longer able to keep their commitment and fulfill the duties of their job description, they should talk to the facilitator, President, or Executive Director as soon as possible.

Thriving Together

"When you become successful and people want your input or your stamp of approval, as a board you've got to be pretty savvy about how to work together and what your process is for coming to consensus or coming to decisions. This is where governance becomes important. You realize, 'that's part of what we do. We have to be good at that.' It's just not enough to do things that are interesting or fun or appealing."

Annan Paterson, Sustainable Novato

Traditionally, the governance committee of a grassroots or non-profit organization recruits new board members and lets them know how the board functions so they can carry out their responsibilities effectively. Other areas of importance include:

- How the board is structured, governs itself and operates
- Making sure the voices of all board members are heard
- Determining board policy on taking an official position for or against an issue, measure or policy
- Determining board policy on protocols for collaborating with other groups
- Determining board policy on sponsoring other groups' events or projects

Any of the procedures, policies and rules set by the board and by which the board governs itself should be recorded as the organization's by-laws. These will serve as the operations manual for your board and traditionally deal briefly with the following:

- Board of Directors roles, duties and terms
- Committees
- Meetings
- Voting
- Conflict of interest
- Fiscal Policies
- Making amendments to the by-laws

Words of Wisdom: Thriving Together

"[Looking] at how the board governs itself and operates has been really important."

Annan Paterson, Sustainable Novato

"We all have a great deal to say, so part of our governance work was to make sure that whenever we consider a decision, or our public position on an issue, every voice gets heard and we fully understand where everyone's coming from before a vote is taken."

Marie Chan, Sustainable Novato

Group Decision-Making

"Decision-making is something that you have to discipline yourselves about. Allow a certain amount of time for discussion, and then go to a vote."

John Schlag, Sustainable Novato

You will be called on to make many decisions as a group. While you will often all agree, there will be times you won't. It is important to put some thought into what kind of mechanism for decision-making will work for your group. Whether by consensus agreement, Roberts Rules of Order and Parliamentary Procedure or majority, you'll save yourselves a lot of time and angst if you agree on this up front.

Allow Time for Discussion Before A Vote

Allowing time for sufficient discussion will lead your board to understand issues more clearly. In the process, it is important to hear from everyone and for each person to be given an equal voice. But be aware that people tend to have a lot to say on any given topic, particularly controversial ones, so it is important to consider how much discussion time you will allocate per person and overall before you come to a vote.

For More info on Consensus Decision-Making, visit:

www.ic.org/pnp/ocac

For More Info on Robert's Rules of Order:

www.robertsrules.org

Find Creative Ways to Conduct Business & Save Time:

Sustainable Marin's board has developed a working style that allows busy members to conduct business as necessary in between board meetings. Says board member John Schlag, *"It's a sort of triage approach."* As issues come up, they identify them as:

1. Items that are administrative and easily taken care of by email, in which case, the board votes by email;

2. Items that clearly require a lot of attention, open discussion, brainstorming and having all board members physically present. These are held for board meetings;

3. Items in the grey area in between. These get considered by board members via email and then either raised up to the status where they need to be discussed at a board meeting, or delegated to particular members to flesh out further then present to the board again for vote by email.

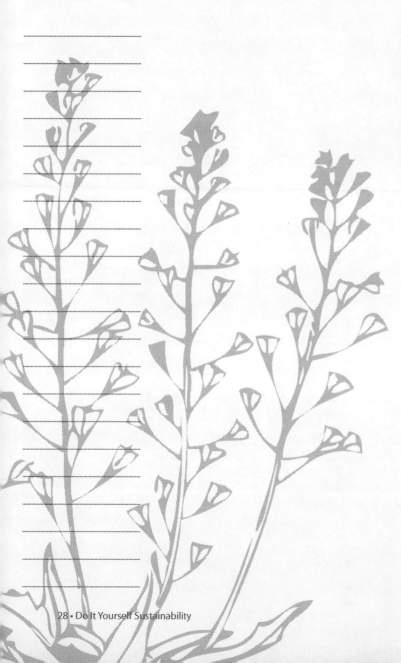

Decision-Making Tool for Managing Board Votes

The board of Sustainable Fairfax often employs the "Gradients of Agreement" process from the book *Facilitators Guide to Participatory Decision-Making* published by San Francisco-based Community at Work (www.communityatwork.com). This process has each board member chart their opinion on a given proposal, giving each a clear voice and often indicating the direction a decision is heading early on.

Example: Instructions for "Gradients of Agreement" Procedure For Reaching Decisions

We will seek to find consensus on all matters before the board, but will resort to a vote if needed for resolution. We believe every voice should be heard before decisions are made.

1. During discussion, anyone can suggest closure, by saying "We seem to be ready to make a proposal." If no objections, then move to # 2. If there is any objection, resume the discussion and repeat #1.

2. Facilitator asks, "Who feels that they can capture the proposal?" Proposal is spoken aloud. Proposal is clarified in open discussion; secretary/scribe captures proposal in writing on a chart. If proposal requires specific action, clarify Who, What & Where. Facilitator asks whether group is ready to take a poll. If ready, move to #3, if not repeat #2.

3. Secretary/scribe draws a line at the bottom of the chart and from left to right and writes down these options:

   1. *"I'm excited."*

   2. *"I like it, but it's not perfect."*

   3. *"It's OK, but I have some concerns."*

   4. *"Pass."*

   5. *"I don't like it, but I understand its value."*

   6. *"I seriously don't like it, but I don't want to hold up the group."*

   7. *"I strongly disagree."*

   8. *"Block."*

4. Each person privately writes down their numerical response to the proposal. All responses are passed to secretary/scribe who then charts them. Facilitator checks with the group to see whether a basic consensus is reached. If so, move to #5. If anyone feels that a decision has not been reached or there is a blocking vote, discussion is reopened or provisions are made to open it at a later date. After three times using the Gradients of Agreement chart, the facilitator will call for a majority vote.

5. The proposal and gradients chart are marked and dated as a conclusive decision.

Your Guiding Light: Determining Your Mission Statement

A good mission statement will elegantly identify the organization's purpose and act as a focus for all of its work. It should be clear, succinct and compelling in order to inspire your board, volunteers, members, subscribers, and community partners. It can also be used to promote your organization and help attract funding. The board should frequently review the mission to insure all of the organization's work is aligned with it.

Here are some examples:

Sustainable Fairfax:

"Sustainable Fairfax supports the philosophy that we must attend to the needs of the present without sacrificing the ability of future generations and the natural world to provide for their own needs. We are a non-profit educational organization providing the infrastructure for all age groups in our community to work together to regenerate and preserve the social, economic and environmental well-being of Fairfax and its sphere of influence."

Sustainable Marin:

"Advance sustainable principles in the County of Marin in the State of California with the goal to transform the region in the areas or environment, economics, and society in to a sustainable community by the year 2040 and beyond."

Sustainable Mill Valley:

"To foster sustainable decision-making throughout Mill Valley, with a focus on promoting the adoption and implementation of public policies that reflect sustainability principles."

Sustainable Novato:

"Our mission is to bring about a healthy and vital environment, self-reliant economy, and inclusive community for the long term."

Sustainable San Rafael:

"Sustainable San Rafael is dedicated to advocacy and community education to help bring about a healthy, balanced and aware society. We are residents and business people organized around the idea that we can and must do more in our own community to fight global warming and encourage more sustainable living. Our primary focus is working with our city and county government to adopt policies that do this, and with our fellow citizens to lead by example."

Board Retreats: Planning & Reflecting on Your Work

Once a year, the board should take one or two days to meet, evaluate the work done over the past year and look ahead to the coming year. This can create a clean slate and allow a clear focus for the year to come. During the retreat, the board may:

- **Honor the work that was done over the past year.** This is a crucial step in any organization of volunteers. Even an act as simple as reading a list of accomplishments out loud can make everyone feel that all their hard work actually had results. This is also a great list to use for fundraising, in a year-end email to members, or to post on the organization's website.

- **Identify the strengths of the organization.** Each year the board changes based on the individuals involved and the organization's strategic initiatives. One year most of your efforts may be focused on fighting a bad practice in the community with lots of good, strong activists standing up and making your organization heard. Another year the focus might be on building something more positive in the community through collaboration with other groups. Whatever the focus, take the time to identify what worked well that year.

- **Brainstorm and problem-solve** regarding organizational development and capacity building. How can you grow your reach?

- **Review the mission statement** to insure that the organization's work continues to be aligned with its purpose.

- **Address and resolve any unresolved issues** that have come up the previous year re: governance, communication, protocols, etc.

- **Determine strategic initiatives** for the next year or look ahead and plan three- or five-year strategic initiatives.

- **Have fun!** Plan a potluck meal and make time to get to know each other and chat about life, not just business. Being socially bonded makes the work more fun and collaboration easier.

Effective Meetings

There is never a shortage of meetings to attend! In addition to your group's board meetings, committee meetings, and meetings for your members and the general public, some people will be attending meetings or hearings on relevant issues held by City Councils, County Supervisors, school boards, utilities districts or Chambers of Commerce. Each committee should determine what kind of time commitment it can realistically manage.

You may start out holding your meetings in people's living rooms and then looking for larger spaces to accommodate more people as you grow. Banks, community centers, churches, like-minded non-profits, schools, town operated facilities, even local businesses will often offer free or low cost meeting space for community groups.

Tips for effective meetings:

- **Agendas, Agendas, Agendas!** People will stop attending meetings if they feel they are consistently unproductive or boring. To avoid this, design an agenda ahead of time with very specific items to be discussed, decisions to be made, and time to be allotted for each item. Include time for issues brought forward by members.

- **Build In Interaction:** Build in a segment that allows for group interaction through meaningful dialogue and input.

- **Ground Rules:** Set some ground rules for the meeting, i.e.; ask everyone to participate, avoid cross-talk, maintain momentum and work for closure.

- **Keep Track of Time:** Set an end time and stick to it, keeping track of time along the way. If the planned time is getting out of hand, ask the group for input to find a resolution.

- **Action Items:** Review all action items and assignments for each committee member.

- **Rotate Facilitator:** Rotate the facilitation of all meetings so everyone gets to experience being a leader.

- **Schedule Next Meeting:** Set the date, time and location for the next meeting and ask each person to commit to being there.

- **Send Out Minutes:** Notes on the meeting should go out to everyone within one week, whether present or not. The easiest way to do this is to have a person take notes directly into an email, highlight action items, and send off at the end of the meeting.

- **End on a Positive Note:** Always attempt to end meetings on a positive note.

Example: Two Meeting Agendas

Board Meeting (Agenda set by President with input from board members with big business items.)

- **Check-in** (say how you are briefly)
- **Announcements**
- **Big Business Items:** Items that have been sent to the facilitator before the meeting which require whole group discussion, decision-making or a vote.
- **Status reports:** Each chair or co-chair reports on their committee's goal and targets, progress on action items, significant events since last meeting, or upcoming events.
- **Old or new business** is brought up for review or set for next meeting.
- **Set next meeting**
- **Check out**

Committee Meeting (Agenda set by chair or co-chair with input from committee members)

- **Check-in**
- **Quick business**
- **First major topic**
- **State meeting's objective**
- **Overview, discussion, plan**
- **Continue until objective is reached**
- **Identify action items**
- **Take a break if needed**
- **Second major topic**
- **State meeting's objective**
- **Overview, discussion, plan**
- **Continue until objective is reached**
- **Identify action items**
- **Review action items**
- **Set next meeting**
- **Check out**

"Your agendas are really important. When you're setting agendas for a meeting, make sure you set time to talk not just about external issues, but about internal issues as well. We look carefully at how we operate as a board, how we communicate, how we are governing ourselves. Because when things get tough or controversial, or if someone has made a mistake or overstepped their bounds, these are the things that you go back to. We also learned to create really tight agendas, and to keep people on time in our meetings"

Kiki LaPorta, Sustainable San Rafael

Board Meetings

A board usually meets once a month to address organizational business, hear reports on committee activities from committee chairs, and determine next steps or actions. The reports serve to make all board members aware of what is going on throughout the organization and create opportunities for cross-committee collaboration.

Executive Board Meetings

Sometimes you'll need to call on the executive board to handle big concerns like major disagreement on an issue, the desire to remove someone from the board, or financial challenges. It is best to have a subcommittee meet first to hash out the challenges and come up with one or two concrete proposals to bring to the board. The board can still weigh in or be allowed to counter propose.

Committee Meetings

Technically these should be held at least once a month to keep the momentum going for the work of each committee, but some may not need to meet as often. It is up to each committee chair to determine how often, where and when their committee will meet based on the committee's focus and activity level. The chair should prepare an agenda for each meeting in advance and keep all committee members informed whether they show up or not.

Membership Meetings/ Meetings for the General Public

Ideally these should be held monthly, as they provide an opportunity to bring in more members, let your community know what you are up to, and offer concrete ways they can participate. Plan these meetings so that they are interesting and dynamic and people will enjoy attending them. Offer them as a forum for community education on a range of sustainability issues. Bring in interesting speakers or experts whenever possible to draw new audience members and raise awareness.

Tips and Logistics: Organizing Meetings for the General Public

Running a good public meeting means managing a lot of logistics. But with good planning and organization you will insure a respectable and professional outcome, and an energized crowd.

Location: Identify location of venue (free or very low cost) and make reservations well in advance to secure. Arrange to get the key and return it when finished.

It is difficult to know in advance how many people will attend, so choose as wisely as you can when securing a venue.

Agenda: Plan an agenda for the meeting.

Designate Roles: You'll need people to staff the sign-in table at the entrance, introduce the agenda, the organization's mission, initiatives and news, and the speaker, cover the refreshments table, and even take photos or video tape the event.

Speaker: Invite and secure an interesting speaker or expert. Be sure to pre-screen so you know he or she will be good and not bore your audience! Offer an honorarium based on donations received at the event.

Capture New Members: Every audience member is a potential new member for your group! Make sure to have clipboards with sign-in sheets at the meeting. Include space to collect name, email address, physical address (or at least the city) and a phone number.

Refreshment: Provide simple refreshments if you like. Make them, buy them or get them donated by a local businesses. If donated, be sure to acknowledge the donors publicly during the meeting.

Materials: Prepare any materials for an information table, such as articles, fact sheets, brochures or flyers.

Advertise: Send email invitations to your member/subscriber list and beyond. Send media alerts to local newspapers and other organizations. Create and strategically post a few signs or flyers around town.

Set-Up and Clean-up: Solicit help from other volunteers in preparing the venue for the meeting, setting up chairs, laying out materials, etc. Make sure you also have help for clean-up so that it is not left to one or two people. Be sure to leave the venue impeccably clean so you will be welcomed back in the future.

Follow Up: Send your attendees a follow-up email acknowledging them for coming and alerting them to any future events. You may even prepare this ahead of time to be sure it goes out immediately following the event.

Goal Setting: Choosing Strategic Initiatives

As you look around at the issues currently facing your community, you may easily become overwhelmed. *Where do we start? How will we make a difference?* This feeling can be compounded by low membership early on and the limited time and energy that members of a volunteer organization will have to offer.

The solution for this is to focus the organization's efforts on a small number of strategic initiatives. Strategic initiatives will provide direction and coherence to everything the organization does in a given year. They should be selected based on the needs of the community as related to the needs of the planet, as well as speak to the passions and interests of the people on your board.

It is best if each if leader or co-leaders are determined for each initiative at the outset. An idea or initiative is only as good as the volunteer willing to take it on.

If you want, survey your community to help you determine your strategic initiatives for the year.

Research First

Before you get too invested in an initiative, do some research on work that might already have been done on it in other parts of the country or the world. In many cases, thanks to the pioneering work of others, you won't have to reinvent the wheel and instead can adopt and adapt campaigns, policies and practices that have already met with success elsewhere.

Find out who else has tackled this initiative. What ordinances or laws have been written and applied in other places that could be adopted locally? What new practices have

Borrow From Others to Make Your Case

You can acquire copies of ordinances, policies and resolutions from other cities to provide to your local government, agencies or school boards as functional examples, then urge them to adopt them as well. Most states have a League of Cities organization that will share this kind of information to influence policy decisions that affect cities.

been implemented? What educational campaigns are already out there to adopt or borrow from? What can be learned from them?

If there is another organization in your area focused on an initiative in which your group is interested, consider working to enhance its efforts rather than reinvent the wheel. But beware that some organizations can be very competitive about limited funding sources and might be offended if you move in on their territory. You can always choose to focus on something you can really make your own.

Design Your Work

Throughout the year, all of the work your group does should be designed based on the focus you've identified with your strategic initiatives. Each major initiative can also have sub-initiatives.

For example:

Climate Change: Can include transportation, electricity generation, energy efficiency education and consultation with businesses and individuals, Cities for Climate Protection campaign, bikeable/walkable communities, Critical Mass rides, Safe Routes to School, solar co-op purchasing groups…

Water: Can include conservation initiatives, rainwater harvesting, greywater, sustainable garden practices, creek restoration, toxics-free creeks via pesticide education or bans…

Food: Can include garden harvest exchanges, community gardens, victory gardens, Permaculture demonstrations, local farms, sustainable organic farms, farmers markets…

Zero Waste: Can include landfill awareness, composting, recycling programs in the schools and city, resource recovery plan, plastic bag bans…

"Every year, one of the fun things we do is a community survey at the Fairfax Eco-Fest. We put up a grid and people put stickers on it to show what areas they're interested in learning about: Food, shopping and eating local, walking or biking, alternative energy, local currency, community gardens, environmental toxins, ride share, green building, water reclamation, community building…"

Pam Hartwell-Herrero, Sustainable Fairfax

Case Study: Sustainable Fairfax's Top 5 Strategic Initiatives and Some Accomplishments

1. CLIMATE CHANGE

Dirty electricity generation and vehicles powered by fossil fuel are major contributors to climate change. To work towards reducing Fairfax's carbon emissions, Sustainable Fairfax brought Cities for Climate Protection and Community Choice Law to the Fairfax Town Council, which became the first in the county to sign on. Community Choice Law has since been embraced as Marin Clean Energy by city and county government throughout Marin County. Marin Clean Energy now procures and provides a choice of thirty to one hundred percent renewable energy for all customers at rates competitive with former monopoly and dirty energy provider, Pacific Gas & Electric.

Sustainable Fairfax also encourages alternative modes of transportation with its Lorax campaign and has worked to increase the number of bike racks in town.

2. WASTE

Because our landfills are filling up and toxic trash is polluting the planet, Sustainable Fairfax wanted to bring awareness to this issue and offer small solutions. They installed recycling bins all around town and established a battery recycling program which has spread throughout the county, where all police stations are now required to have battery drop off receptacles.

Sustainable Fairfax demonstrates five different composting methods in its Sustainability Center garden. It facilitated the first plastic-free farmers market, and put the first plastic bag ban in the country on the ballot. The ballot measure won seventy-nine percent of the vote and inspired the county to adopt an ordinance banning single use plastic grocery bags and charging five cents per paper bag used.

Sustainable Fairfax consults with the Town of Fairfax on contracts with its garbage haulers and has helped to slow the landfill expansion. It also offers community education on reducing waste through smart shopping and provides affordable reusable bags. Its Zero Waste initiative works to reduce waste at town events.

3. WATER

Marin County has seasonal rain with regular drought conditions, and with this comes a responsibility to use water wisely.

At the same time, Fairfax is situated in a flood zone, and flood events periodically cause major damage to homes, local businesses, and town resources.

Sustainable Fairfax has created a water reclamation and conservation demonstration project at its Sustainability Center that can be incorporated into any property. The project models rainwater catchment, drought tolerant plantings, a rain garden, and low water irrigation systems. It encourages the reduction of non-permeable surfaces on any property to

help prevent water from entering the storm drains too quickly, contributing to flooding downstream.

In 2010, Sustainable Fairfax was chosen for a pilot program funded by the municipal water district to see how much they could help Fairfax residents increase water conservation. In one year, residents successfully reduced water usage five percent more than their neighboring communities.

4. FOOD

In this country, most supermarket food travels over a thousand miles from farm to table. Agribusiness farms that use petroleum-based pesticides and fertilizers are some of the most polluting businesses on the planet.

Sustainable Fairfax encourages community members to grow their own food, know their local farmers and vote with their fork. It works to educate shoppers by partnering with local organizations like Marin Master Gardeners, Marin Farmers Market and Marin Organic. It has hosted a 100-mile food challenge, has an active seed library and exchange, offers education on raising chickens, and has a Victory Garden Project to encourage participation in creating the most bountiful foodshed possible!

5. LOCALIZATION

While many small towns have lost their character and local jobs to Big Box stores, the Town of Fairfax remains unique in that it has refused Big Box stores.

It has been shown that when money is spent locally it stays in the community and brings with it prosperity. This contributes to the creation of a thriving, self-reliant community that provides needed goods and services to community members and manages its resources sustainably.

In a survey of Fairfax shoppers, Sustainable Fairfax found that the only things that can't be purchased in Fairfax are iPods, phones and computers. Sustainable Fairfax has worked closely with the Chamber of Commerce and many local businesses to shine a light on businesses embodying sustainability. Sustainable Fairfax also co-sponsored a Green Chamber mixer that was instrumental in bringing Green Business certification to more local businesses, and introduced the BALLE and CittaSlow programs to Fairfax, as well as a local currency called the FairBuck. [To learn more about the FairBuck, see *Case Study: Local Currency* in Appendix B.]

Examples of Existing Campaigns, Initiatives and Ordinances:

350.org (www.350.org). A global grassroots movement to solve the climate crisis.

Business Alliance for Local Living Economies (BALLE - www.livingeconomies.org). An organization that catalyzes, strengthens and connects networks of locally owned independent businesses dedicated to building strong Local Living Economies.

Ban the Bottle (www.banthebottle.net). A campaign to ban the plastic bottle.

New Rules Project (www.newrules.org/policy-areas)
A program of the Institute for Local Self-Reliance that brings fresh new policy solutions to communities and states.

ICLEI Cities for Climate Protection campaign (www.iclei.org). An association of local and regional governments committed to sustainable development.

Marin Clean Energy (www.marincleanenergy.info). A public entity that procures renewable energy and partners with existing utility for energy delivery and customer service.

Plastic bag bans (www.plasticbaglaws.org/legislation). A resource for municipalities considering local ordinances banning the commercial use of plastic bags.

Pesticide bans (www.pesticidefreezone.org). National and local resources for reducing the use of pesticides in schools, municipalities, and homes.

Safe Routes to School (www.saferoutesinfo.org). A national program encouraging children to safely walk and bike to school.

Common Threads: Goal Setting ~ Determining Strategic Objectives

- Focus your work, efforts and time by determining your strategic initiatives. Don't bite off more than you can chew!

- Carefully select two to five strategic initiatives per year.

- Research, Research, Research.

- Borrow from the work of others who've preceded you.

- Develop action plans and form proposals based on your initiatives.

- Plan ahead, and accept there will be work left over for next year.

- Prepare to be caught up by an issue you didn't foresee.

- Find the balance between driving an issue and responding to crisis.

Words of Wisdom: Goal Setting ~ Determining Strategic Objectives

"The capacity to take on a few more things is always a function of talent that you are able to attract to the organization and the interests that people have. Sure, there are a lot more things we could do, but the whole idea is to have a set of strategic initiatives to focus us on just doing a few things well, things that have a real payoff, and not get distracted into feel-good projects or green-washing projects. Let's try to focus on realities and try to do real things and build institutions."

Ed Mainland, Sustainable Novato

CHAPTER THREE

Find Your Community Partners! Building Positive Relationships

"The whole model of sustainability is: No one's in this alone; we're all in this together."

Annan Paterson, Sustainable Novato

"It's all about the relationships."

Kiki LaPorta, Sustainable San Rafael

A cornerstone of your work will be building lasting, positive relationships within your community, based on collaboration and mutual respect. Seeking these relationships out and nurturing them will enable your organization to bring measurable and meaningful changes to your community. Over time, sustainability will become more and more a part of the community-wide conversation and framework.

Potential partners include:

- Local Government: City Council, Community Planning, Services and Development departments, Public Works, Redevelopment agencies, city staff
- Public utility agencies and special districts, i.e.; water, waste management, sanitation
- School boards, staff, teachers, and students
- Other non-profits and grassroots organizations
- Local businesses and Chambers of Commerce
- Neighborhood groups
- Rotary and other traditional organizations
- Religious institutions
- Individuals who are respected leaders or holders of the history of the community

Reach Out for Guidance

This is a great way to begin to establish relationships. Make personal contact with County Supervisors, City Council members, planning commissioners, school board members, leaders of other like-minded organizations, experts in fields such as renewable energy, sustainable planning, or affordable housing. Offer to take them out for a cup of coffee or go to their turf, sit down, ask questions, and just chat with them. Let them know about your newly forming organization and its mission, and that you value their expertise and guidance as you get started. Take their advice to heart.

Form Coalitions with Like-Minded Groups

The old way of doing things didn't include big picture thinking or taking into account how all the parts relate and who else might already be doing work relevant to yours. In the sustainability framework, everything and everyone is connected. Therefore, connect yourselves! Identify and work towards your common goals with a diverse group of like-minded organizations. Look around to see who might already be focusing on some of the areas that are important to your organization's initiatives and make connections with them. Invite them to come speak at your meetings and events or co-host a class. Together you represent greater numbers, and your collective voice and resulting power will be stronger.

"All of those issues that impact environmental health and sustainable communities do not exist in a vacuum. It's not just about housing. It's not just about transportation. It's not just about green building or limiting toxins in our daily lives. It's about how that's all connected. Over the last couple of years, I've been on a pointed

mission to find those groups and discover how we might support each other. These kinds of alliances need to be continually built and nurtured. You don't always work together on projects; it depends on what the particular organization focuses on at the moment. But certainly when there is overlap, we should be able to not reinvent the wheel, but support each other."

–Marie Chan, Sustainable Novato

Choose Partners Wisely

When considering joining forces with other organizations that share common goals or values, choose wisely. Protect your organization's reputation and integrity in the community. Beware of organizations or their members who may be consistently antagonistic, angry, or combative in meetings with "the opposition." If this seems likely, remain independent from the organization in question, but continue to work towards your shared goals. Decision-makers are much more likely to invite you into the room if you are pragmatic and reasonable to work with.

Nurture Your Relationships

Put energy into nurturing your relationships with community partners by speaking with them regularly, emailing them, asking their advice, and attending their events. Invite them to your events and general meetings consistently. Go on hikes together, have coffee, get to know their families. Making this extra effort can bring all kinds of benefits over the long term, including finding new, like-minded friends and 'angels' to champion your cause and help advance it.

Tailor Your Approach in Every Instance

Try not to greet each new individual or organization with a one-size-fits-all approach. Instead, pay careful attention to who they are and how they function. Find out how much each person you meet already knows about your topic or initiative before you make any assumptions about them. Let this guide you in tailoring your

About Complaining

There is a tendency for people who speak at open time during City Council, school board or other meetings to complain about all kinds of issues. This negative drone can be off-putting and not a great way to start or nurture a relationship. Offering a positive solution and being willing to help move toward that solution goes a long way.

approach with them and look for ways to create win-win relationships and situations.

"How do I make this a win-win situation for both of us? I understand where you're coming from. I know you need help and you would like me to help you get to where you want to be. How can we help each other? It can be as simple and as superficial a relationship as that, or it can be a much deeper relationship like ones we've developed with other organizations."

Marie Chan, Sustainable Novato

Case Study: A Medley on Nurturing Relationships

In their early days, members of Sustainable San Rafael personally invited two San Rafael City Council members to attend a board meeting. To their delight, they accepted. When asked for advice about how best to proceed with the idea of developing a green building ordinance for the city, the Council Members readily offered their guidance. They followed up by directing their Community Development and Planning Department Director to hold a study session with members of Sustainable San Rafael. The input and participation of these Council Members helped pave the way for the organization's tremendous success with that initiative. *"Those relationships really go a*

long way," said Kiki LaPorta of Sustainable San Rafael, *"You can understand how lobbying and PACs work…"*

Members of Sustainable Mill Valley attended many City Council and Planning Commission meetings to provide input and insure that sustainability became a consistent part of the conversation. The City Council and staff got to know and like them, even calling on them from time to time to weigh in on various issues.

"It makes a difference when [members of city government] respect you and think that you're worth listening to," said Marie Kerpan of Sustainable Mill Valley, *"You really have the ear of the people that are making decisions. You have to work the politics. If you don't, then you're not as effective."*

Sustainable Fairfax has had the rare pleasure of having a Town Council known for its progressive and green politics. Says Pam Hartwell-Herrero, Executive Director of Sustainable Fairfax:

"We're so lucky. We don't spend any time fighting. Our Town Council loves us and we have close relationships with just about every single Council Member. They come to our events. They speak at our events. They reach out to us and seek our advice. They like what we do and believe that we're easy to work with. We're not an 'agro grassroots group.' We'll definitely tell them if we're

not happy about something that they're doing, but we're much more interested in collaborating with them on things."

But this doesn't mean they haven't put energy into those relationships:

"But it's not just luck, we give them our time and energy and we do really great things in the town that they sometimes can't do. They're sometimes limited by staff, liability, litigation or other issues, and they're delighted that we're not. For example, our policy Chair/Vice President worked with the Council on negotiating the garbage contract between the waste haulers and the town. So, we can sometimes be a little edgier and enter into negotiations, and if the town really wants something but they're a little bit afraid to ask for it, we can ask for it and we don't have to be afraid."

Common Threads: Find Your Community Partners! ~ Building Positive Relationships

- Seek guidance and advice.
- Approach all people with respect and find common ground.
- Tailor your approach for each person and group or organization.
- Form coalitions with like-minded groups, but choose wisely.

- Focus on solutions. People and groups who only emphasize others' mistakes don't get invited in to talk about solutions.
- Make a commitment to build and sustain positive relationships that serve your organization's goals and values.
- Be collaborative and inclusive.

Words of Wisdom: Find Your Community Partners! ~ Building Positive Relationships

"Approach all people with respect. This is the number one rule. Each time you approach someone you will want and need to work with, consider that while they may not agree with you at the outset, nor when you're finished, at the end of the day, it's not personal. You can still speak passionately and persuasively. Use each meeting as an opportunity to share ideas, educate people and advance sustainability in your town. Know that many times people will have little to no prior knowledge of what you speak of."

Marie Chan, Sustainable Novato

CHAPTER FOUR

Go Forth and Make Positive Change! Advocating and Educating in Your Community

"We work from the top down and bottom up at the same time: effecting change at the legislative, municipal level which imposes a framework on the way we live, as well as educating people in the community."

Kiki LaPorta, Sustainable San Rafael

Which Comes First, Advocating for Good Policy or Educating Your Community?

If your group is like the five featured in this guidebook, your work will likely be a mix of advocating for sustainable policies for your city government, schools and businesses, and providing sustainability education for the community so that people can make informed choices in their lives and support your initiatives. Picking either advocacy or community education as a single focus is sort of like asking 'which came first, the chicken or the egg?' You can't really have one without the other, and they both influence each other. Getting your city to adopt good sustainable policies makes a real difference. But, if there are only five of you trying to move an unwilling City Council you may have a hard time doing so. This is where community education comes in.

Offering sustainability education to your community through talks, classes or workshops will also make your work more visible, bring more people in to support your cause and build a constituency. All of this gives your organization more clout with city government, public agencies, schools and businesses. It also helps bring awareness and legitimacy to issues of sustainability from the global, down to the local and personal level, and helps community members see more and more how their personal choices have an impact on their local and global communities.

Creating Meaningful Change in Community Policy and Practices

"We felt we could have the biggest impact in terms of making change by getting to the people who are making policy."

Kiki LaPorta, Sustainable San Rafael

Helping your city, business community or schools create and adopt policies that contribute to a more sustainable future is an important piece in turning the cogs of the wheel towards change. However, city staff is often short of the time, money or vision needed to do the kind of research and legwork necessary to bring about new policy. They can definitely benefit from your educated input and energy. Beware though, policy change frequently implies dealing with "politics." Council and board members who are serving at the will of the people can become defensive or closed to you if they feel they are under attack.

Knowing how to play the game with integrity and finesse is key, and being in the room when decisions are being made is much better than simply making angry comments during open time at public meetings. Policy change can often be a painstakingly slow process due to the limitations mentioned above along with government bureaucracy. If you enter into this work with this awareness, you are more likely to pace yourselves appropriately and meet with success.

Start With Your Own Education

Whether you are working with your school board, City Council or a public agency, when you want to see sustainable policies and practices adopted, you need to make your case intelligently and engage your audience. In most cases your initiatives will be complex in nature. Take the time to study their complexities and understand all sides of the issue. Think about why the "other side" is taking the position it is. All of this preparation will allow you to

thoughtfully discuss the issue or initiative, and make powerful presentations, arguments and comments.
It will also gain you tremendous respect.

Non-profit Neutrality

Non-profits must remain neutral in regards to endorsing candidates or political parties based on 501(c)(3) rulings, or risk losing non-profit status. They can however endorse ballot measures and do voter education as long as it is equal opportunity and fair. Individuals that are associated with organizations will often endorse specific candidates but must require the use of a disclaimer that says, "the endorsement of this individual does not indicate the endorsement of the organization."

Visit www.nonprofitvote.org for more information.

Who Will You Need to Influence?

Who will you need to influence? Who can be persuaded? Who needs to hear your side? Whose influence do you need? Elected officials? Public agency or private entity? Business owners? School boards? And what will you be asking of them? What do you have to offer them? Will you be calling them into action of some kind? Asking them to support your initiative with a vote? Looking for them to advise you? Requesting they help you network? Looking for funding?

Know all of this and more ahead of time, then try to set up one-on-one meetings with key players. Send them limited and appropriate briefing materials prior to your meeting. Whenever possible, provide solid examples and models of successful ordinances, projects or campaigns from other municipalities to help make your case and provide a framework on which to build. Find local experts on your issue and ask them to contribute their expertise to your cause by joining you in meetings, or providing letters or other documentation. Have members of the local business community, or parents in a school district with mutual desires contribute their voices as well.

When you have the opportunity to speak with decision or policy-makers, always ascertain their position on your issue right away. If it is the same as yours, find out what you can do to strengthen support for it. If it is different than yours or they are undecided, try to open a dialogue so you can better understand each other. Find out what information or show of public support would help them change their position, then follow through by doing what you can to facilitate it happening.

Seek Collaboration

Approach all players with the spirit of collaboration, always looking for ways to work together to bring about sustainable policies and practices. With this attitude, your input is much more likely to be welcomed in the decision-making process.

Power in Numbers

If your group only consists of a few active members, don't highlight the small numbers in meetings, print or hearings. But, if you have built a list of several hundred or thousand subscribers, be sure to let people know. In many cases these kinds of numbers will carry weight with elected officials or others and help influence their decisions.

Demonstrate Cost-Benefit

More often than not, your proposals will be met with resistance or concern based on short-term, bottom-line thinking. Try to meet this kind of thinking by demonstrating the longer-term cost-benefit of your proposal. Do your research as best you can and document it using real numbers that reflect both the internalized costs of doing business-as-usual, and the externalized costs to the local and/or global community. Contrast this information by showing how your proposal will actually save money and resources, even if it is over the long term.

Get on the Record

Get your proposals or concerns on the record whenever possible. Do this by getting on the agenda or speaking during open time at important meetings. This is a necessary part of public policy making and serves to document the process officially.

Work for Vs. Fight Against

Whenever possible, be the group advocating for a positive future rather than fighting against a bad practice or policy. Being in a battle mode all the time will not endear you to your "foes" and it will lead you to burnout sooner. Choose your battles wisely, focus on creative solutions, and seek allies instead of enemies.

Avoid Antagonism

When things get heated you can be strong, make your point and disagree, but avoid being antagonistic. This is one way to protect your organization's integrity and leave the door open for future collaboration. This doesn't mean you have to back down from a conflict, but try to be the "fist in the velvet glove" if you find yourself involved in one. Use diplomacy, clarity and finesse to make your argument and hopefully bring people around to your position. Show that you are willing to work collaboratively so that you can be a part of the decision-making.

"We saw early on the importance of getting in with the City Council and having them know that we were collaborative. We felt strongly that there was no point in being antagonist, which I think was a very important thing because so many environmental groups get antagonistic. We really worked hard at building relationships. At first [the City Council was] antagonistic toward us, so we had to really push in a gentle and diplomatic way to get heard, but we did get heard."

Marie Kerpan, Sustainable Mill Valley

Follow Relevant Timelines

Be sure to get in on the policy change process as soon as possible. Keep track of when significant meetings are being held, official comments are due, or important votes are taking place and be prepared for them. Always ask if you can meet with members of the deciding body before the meeting. It can be very frustrating to come and speak your mind during public comment time and not feel heard because a Council or board has already determined its position. You may often need to attend multiple meetings to voice your concerns effectively, so be sure you attend the right ones. Attending early meetings is always better than only showing up for the last meeting on the subject.

Find Your Public Speaking Voice

To be an effective speaker, you will want to prepare thoughtful, to the point, articulate speeches. It is best not to complain angrily, be overly emotional, or tell people they are wrong. This is a sure way to shut people down and turn them off to collaborating with you. There may be times when it is appropriate to let someone know you are disappointed in a choice they've made, or to challenge an idea they've presented. In these cases, carefully choose how to communicate so as not to burn any bridges. You may want to start by attending a meeting where you are happy with what the board or Council has done and thank them publicly for doing such a good job. The people who serve on councils and boards are often trying to do the right thing. They appreciate receiving praise as much as the rest of us.

Over time and with experience you will become more at ease with public speaking. You may also grow comfortable going into meetings without a prepared speech and instead improvising once you've had an opportunity to hear what other speakers have said. This way you can cover any points that haven't been made, or respond to points with which you disagree.

Customarily, each speaker will be limited to two to three minutes, so prepare your thoughts in advance, and rehearse at least a little, as you will find that this time will go by very quickly and you will be asked to stop at or just beyond the time limit.

Public Speaking Tips

- Know who your audience is and address them politely.
- Determine whether you are there to educate or persuade your audience.
- Begin with your name, where you live and the organization with which you are affiliated.
- Try opening with a focus on your audience (perhaps by acknowledging positively something someone has done).
- State your purpose or objective briefly.
- Avoid being adversarial. Be collaborative in nature instead.
- Make your case using a maximum of three key points.
- Include specific facts, stories, quotes or visuals whenever possible.
- Conclude with a brief summary and a call to action. Let your audience know why it's a good idea for them to do what you are asking.

Ask Your Members to Take Action Where it Counts

"Because [initially] we were advocacy-focused, we didn't have a need for a lot of membership, although we would ask our adherents to come to City Council meetings to speak, to stand up, or to at least be acknowledged as members of Sustainable San Rafael to lend weight and leverage to our statements to the City Council."

Kiki LaPorta, Sustainable San Rafael

Depending on the issue your group is addressing at any given point, you will at times want to call on your membership and newsletter subscribers to take some action that will help move things forward. It may be to sign a petition, send an email or letter of support or opposition, make a phone call to an elected official, show up at a meeting and be a body in the room or speak.

Many issues are decided on the sheer volume of communications received from constituents or community stakeholders. If you play your cards right, you can make a friend on the City Council or staff who will report back to you on the general numbers of letters, calls or emails coming in so you know how effective you're being, and if you need to push your membership for more participation.

But how do you move your members and subscribers to take action? Most people are busy and their time is limited, so the easier you make it for them to participate, the more likely they will. Make sure you are clear about what you want them to do and why. No matter what the action is, always try to provide people with as much advance notice and information as possible along with a follow-up reminder as important deadlines approach so they can participate in whatever way works best for them. Some kind of participation is better than none at all.

You can also reach out to other groups and organizations with which you are aligned and ask them to encourage their members to participate. When doing so, always offer prepared messages, letters, petitions, etc. so that they can easily forward them on to their membership.

Send a Letter or Fax

Offer pre-written letters for people to download from your website or copy from an email, or have hard copies available for people to sign when you're tabling at farmers markets or other events. Personalized letters are always far more effective than form letters but a form letter is better than no letter at all. Either way,

letters should be brief and to the point (usually no longer than one page) and include the following information:

- Sender's name, address, and phone number
- The issue stated as clearly and positively as possible
- Sender's position on the issue and why it is important to them
- How the issue will affect the sender, and/or the sender's city, school or community
- The action the sender would like the decision-maker to take

Make a Phone Call

Phone calls are also an effective way to contact policy-makers. Callers should briefly provide the following information during the call:

- Caller's name, address, and phone number
- The issue stated briefly
- The action the caller would like the decision-maker to take

Send an Email

Just like a letter, you can send a pre-written email message people can copy and paste to send on their own, or ask them to compose their own. Provide all necessary contact information (after double-checking to insure it is correct!).

Sign a Petition

Have petitions available for people to sign when you are tabling at farmers markets or other events.

Show Up at an Important Public Meeting

Don't be surprised if you get a low turnout. *"Sometimes we've put out an alert and we've gotten very minimal response,"* says Sue Spofford of Sustainable San Rafael. Be sure to provide plenty of notice and a reminder or two.

"In each case of our success, it was about finding an angel among the elected politicians and having them advance [the cause]."

Ed Mainland, Sustainable Novato

Common Threads: Advocating for Meaningful Change in Community Policy and Practices

- Start with your own education. Do your research and become as expert on the subject as possible.

- One-on-one meetings with local government, school board officials or business leaders can be quite effective. Prepare briefing documents as necessary.

- Whenever possible, bring experts in to help you make your case.

- Invite members of the local business community who want what you want to participate.

- Partner with other organizations interested in your issue.

- Offer to help make it happen in whatever way needed, then follow through.

- Be collaborative and seek solutions.

- Find ways to work well with others, even if you disagree.

- Be a good winner and a good loser. Your adversary on one issue could be your ally on the next one.

- Demonstrate cost-benefit.

- Get on the record.

- Know your timeline and be on top of it. Show up at all relevant meetings.

- Get comfortable with public speaking.

- Persist, persist, persist.

- Diplomacy, diplomacy, diplomacy.

- Have patience. It can be a painstakingly slow process.

- When an official votes your way, always share your appreciation.

Words of Wisdom: Advocating for Meaningful Change in Community Policy and Practices

"One of the things we've learned is you go make your case and let go of the outcome. You may not win the first time around but you keep chipping away. It's a mistake to give up because you don't think you can win. You never know what kind of an impact you can have."

Marie Kerpan, Sustainable Mill Valley

"The issues are very complicated and I'm very aware of the political ramifications. I can see that these are not evil people on the "other side." They have jobs to protect, budget and manpower limitations they have to deal with. We try to move forward despite all of these limitations."

Marie Chan, Sustainable Novato

Educate to Inspire: Bringing Your Community Into the Action

"It's hard when you're always fighting, when it's all about policy and advocacy. It's such a huge benefit to have the community education piece because then you [naturally] build a constituency. Because we have a constituency, people listen to us, people like us, and if you're an elected official, you'd better be willing to work with us or watch out."

Pam Hartwell-Herrero, Sustainable Fairfax

When you hold events to educate and inspire your community, you plant seeds and ignite people in a way that can be infectious. They often return home and share new ideas and enthusiasm with their family, friends and neighbors, further spreading the seeds. Sometimes they get so fired up they identify relevant projects within the community go to work on them independently.

Try a variety of offerings to appeal to a broader audience. If you find out what interests members of your community and offer it to them, they will show up. Once you've captured their interest, you can invite them to become subscribers, and easily keep them up to date on future events, local issues and important actions they can take to support your initiatives.

Consider partnering with existing non-profits on these kinds of events. Partners may even provide the activity and teaching while your organization acts as host, linking the activity to the larger concept of sustainability. Try asking the Conservation Corps to work with you on a recycling project, or finding a local sustainable farm to tour. Ask a creek restoration organization to lead a creek walk, or look to the local waste haulers to provide a tour of their facility.

Some ways to deliver sustainability education to your community:

- General Public Meetings
- Community Forums
- Public Access television broadcasts
- Film nights with speakers
- Lectures and panels with noted locals and experts
- Classes/hands-on workshops
- Field trips
- Tours of demonstration projects
- Neighborhood canvassing
- Book signing events
- Voter education via panels or candidate surveys
- Information tables at farmers markets, fairs and other events

Open Meetings for the General Public

"If you want attendance, you have to offer information that people want to have. That way they'll feel that even if they don't know anyone there, they'll gain some information to take home."

Sue Spofford, Sustainable San Rafael

If possible, open meetings should be offered monthly for your members and the general public. This will give you a consistent presence in the community as well as regular opportunities to gain new members. Meetings can be run by your core members and cover your sustainability initiatives and related information as you see fit.

Remember to keep your meetings interesting and dynamic so audience members will return with their friends and neighbors. Consider inviting local experts or other interesting members of the community to speak each month. Choose people whose expertise links elegantly to one or more of your strategic initiatives. Not only will they draw interest to your event, but they'll often attract their own audience. Pairing a speaker with an educational film related to your initiatives can be another good strategy.

Ask for a suggested donation of whatever amount you think is appropriate for your community. Funds collected can go towards an honorarium for the speaker, to pay for the space, or to purchase refreshments.

Community Forums

Sustainable Novato has become known for its community forums. At each forum, a panel of experts speaks on topics related to Sustainable Novato's strategic initiatives. Initially, Sustainable Novato members who had become quasi-experts through their own research populated the panels. But as the forums quickly gained respect across the community, they began to attract esteemed experts.

Vet Your Speakers

Be sure to vet your speakers. They should be interesting and dynamic in some way in order to engage your audience so they'll come back in the future and bring their friends. Avoid dull, droning speakers who lean on PowerPoint presentations that lack pictures. People want to be inspired.

The forums act as a kind of reality check, reporting the current state of affairs regarding the evening's subject and offering ideas about sustainable solutions. They share proven solutions other communities have employed and examine how Novato residents might influence their community to adopt similar solutions.

Through a partnership with the local public access television channel, the forums are videotaped and televised locally, then rebroadcast over a period of two to three months. This broadens their reach and further disseminates the information.

"Our forums are our signature form of public outreach. They require a massive amount of work to organize, and the level of expertise of our panelists and their renown just continues to grow. And people, fortunately for us, are very happy to participate."

Marie Chan, Sustainable Novato

In addition to the panel of speakers, local organizations with a vested interest in the forum's topics are invited to host information tables and have representatives available to speak to community members for the first thirty minutes of the evening. Subscribers and members of these organizations often attend, bringing Sustainable Novato potential new members.

The panel speaks for sixty minutes, and is followed by a thirty-minute question and answer period. Light refreshment is provided, often donated by local business or organizations (be sure to acknowledge them publicly in some way and encourage community members to support them). A five-dollar donation is requested, though no one is turned away for lack of funds. The forums are very well attended and their audiences continue to grow.

"When we started putting on community forums [it] was kind of a leap for our organization, but something that we really enjoyed. It was a low budget item that brought us a lot of attention and a lot of audience and volunteers as a result because were able to do it through our local public access television station. [The forums] really mobilized our board, our volunteers, and the greater community, too."

Annan Paterson, Sustainable Novato

A Sampling of Sustainable Novato's forums:

Creating Sustainable Communities
A Nexus Of Sustainability Ideas: Climate change, transportation, green building, and housing. Planning, walking, biking, pedestrian pathways, improvement of air quality, all of these things as well as reduction of toxics in green building materials come to play in this one forum.

Green Schools
Climate change and environmental toxins threaten our children's health and future well being. Green schools can create a healthier learning environment, raise test scores, increase attendance, save school districts money in the long run, and reduce global warming impact.

Thinking Outside the (Big) Box, Strategies For A Strong Local Economy
Learn how the principles of sustainability apply to Novato's community, businesses and local economy, and why the big box Home Depot, poised to set up shop in Novato, is not a good idea.

Rethinking Waste: Alternatives to Redwood Landfill
Examines the proposed expansion of Novato's Redwood Landfill and how it could impact Novato and the County of Marin. Discusses safer and healthier alternatives, including Marin County's goals for Zero Waste, prolonging the Landfill's useful life by shrinking the volume of the waste stream, and returning composted green waste to the land, not the dump.

Town Clean Energy Forum
Under State law, local governments can choose the fuels and facilities providing their electricity through a new kind of Community Choice Electricity Aggregation (CCA) "buyer's cooperative," and take charge of their own energy future by contracting with licensed "electric service providers." Learn about the opportunities available to Novato through CCA.

Classes and Workshops

"We offer cutting edge technology from one hundred years ago."

Pam Hartwell-Herrero, Sustainable Fairfax

Sustainable Fairfax holds at least one fun, informative event per month and covers a range of topics. Participants are asked to pay a small fee, which allows Sustainable Fairfax to pay an honorarium to the experts and professionals they invite to teach. Classes and workshops run two to three hours and combine practical information with hands-on experience. Participants often leave with something they've made as well as a personal connection to sustainability, hands-on experience and some new skills.

Some of the popular workshops that have been offered are:

- Rainwater Harvesting & Blue Building with Brock Dolman

- Green Halloween

- Post Carbon: The Local Impact of Climate Change and Peak Oil

- A Wild Harvest Walk

- What to Drive, If You Must

- Detox Your Home

- Dig a Rain Garden

- Build a Cob Oven

- Climate Change in the Garden, with Penny Livingston-Stark

- Make Your Mom a Wormbin

- Rethinking Plastics-Rethinking Our Lives, with Green Sangha

- Where Will Our Trash Go?

- Art into Action, with Nature Sculptor Zach Pine

- Planning a Community Like You Plan a Garden, with James Stark

- A 100-Mile Food Challenge, in collaboration, with Marin Organic and Good Earth Natural Foods

Once, after receiving a sizeable grant, Sustainable Fairfax hired a Permaculture expert to lead a workshop over eight weekends. During that time, participants designed and transformed the backyard of the Sustainability Center into the amazing demonstration garden it is today.

Tours of Relevant Projects and Facilities

Another great way to attract people is by sponsoring tours of local projects that demonstrate sustainability principles. You can tour the local landfill to learn where waste goes, visit a collection of local sustainably grown gardens, or visit

an organic farm. Visit people making change in their own backyards by growing food, raising chickens, using greywater "laundry to landscape" or collecting rainwater. In the Transition movement (www.transitionnetwork.org) this is called "tapping your local genius."

Again, you can ask participants to pay a small fee to support the work of your organization or to pay the person leading the tour.

Farmers Markets, Fairs and Other Events

This is a great way to make personal contact with a large swath of the

community and garner visibility for your organization. You will also tend to find an audience that is very likely ripe for the sustainability conversation.

Get permission from organizers to set up a table, then provide engaging information and displays. Personally invite people to attend events, join your organization, and subscribe to its newsletter. Design activities that are fun for the entire family. For example, Sustainable Fairfax provides weekly activities from making shopping bags out of old t-shirts, to sharing alternatives to plastic storage, to demonstrating healthy recipes using local, organic products. Each week, shoppers are reminded by Sustainable Fairfax to make every Wednesday a "Green Wednesday" by shopping locally, riding a bike or walking to the market, bringing their own bags, and getting to know people in the community.

If you follow this model, people will seek out your table week after week just to see what's new.

Voter Education

If your city is holding an election for seats on the City Council or another public office, your organization can help ensure they are filled by people who champion the principles of sustainability. Create a set of sustainability-themed questions for candidates to answer and let them know

you will be publishing their responses on your website and in local newspapers. This can make sustainability a central theme in the race and help identify the best candidates for the job.

Inviting candidates to speak or debate in voter education forums your organization sponsors can also be tremendously effective. As sustainability organizations gain more visibility and respect in their communities, candidates know that they will be well served to participate if they hope to have a chance at winning the election.

Sometimes an election season requires walking neighborhoods and speaking directly with neighbors. While this option is time intensive, it can be a very effective opportunity to do high impact one-to-one education, as well as bring in new members. It is a good idea to hand out a postcard, pamphlet, door hanger, or flyer that covers the most vital information. You can also create an action-oriented piece, such as a messaged post card for people to sign and send in to their City Council or County Supervisor. [See Appendix B, *Case Study: Neighborhood Canvassing, Marin Clean Energy,* for a detailed case study on this topic.]

Community Parades

Get creative, have fun and be visible in your community by joining local parades. Use a float or just carry signs and smiles as an enjoyable way to get the message out about your organization and sustainability principles.

For example, in preparation for the Mill Valley Centennial parade and celebration, Sustainable Mill Valley got together with local artists and created large cardboard blocks (around six feet tall and two feet wide) painted with different local scenes and messages about sustainability on all

sides. On one side was a big footprint and the question *"How big is your ecological footprint?"* On another was a map of the local watershed showing its creeks like the fingers of a hand. Members of Sustainable Mill Valley crafted a short and simple 'choreography' featuring the blocks and presented a mini sustainability seminar in the town square following the parade. Member Marie Kerpan says, *"We use every opportunity to educate, whether it be whimsical or serious or political."*

Other Inventive Ways to Get the Word Out and Inspire

Look for places around your community where you might set up temporary or permanent displays. Public facilities such as libraries, schools or city buildings often have large bulletin boards or display cases that you might be able to occupy for a period of time. Create displays that are visually interesting, well researched and supply easily accessible information.

Words of Wisdom: Educate to Inspire

"Talk to people about [the issues] in a way that makes them accessible, so they can make informed decisions in their own lives about what's important. It's not about what's right and what's wrong. It's about having the information to decide for yourself, because every family's different; their circumstances are different, and their health concerns are different."

Marie Chan, Sustainable Novato

Be in the Public Eye! Getting the Word Out about Your Organization, Events and Initiatives

Publicizing your work is crucial if you want to promote sustainable policy and practices, build your membership, and strengthen your voice and visibility in the community. Select one or two people in your organization to head up this effort consistently, as it can be easy to let this aspect slide if you are all focused on big initiatives. You will find the pay off to be well worth the effort.

Early Visibility: Create a Web Presence

As soon as you can, launch a website. This is an important way to provide your community with access to information about your organization's mission and strategic initiatives. Your website should also provide an opportunity for people to join your subscriber list and become volunteers or members. You may also want to include a secure option for electronic donations. Consider putting up resources, articles and tips for sustainable living, as well as actions people can take to support sustainable policy and practices in your city, school districts and public agencies. If possible, include a calendar of upcoming events and important

meetings and keep it up to date. Consider posting biographies or testimonials from your board or committee members that focus on what personally makes them passionate about what they do.

Here are some examples:

www.sustainablefairfax.org
www.sustainablemarin.org
www.sustainablemillvalley.org
www.sustainablenovato.org
www.sustainablesanrafael.org

Building a website from scratch can represent some expense if you do not have a website designer on your team who is willing to donate his or her services. Thankfully, there are several free online resources that make website building surprisingly easy, and even offer free website hosting. Just having basic word processing skills can be enough to put together an attractive, informative website. You will still have purchase your website domain name for a small annual fee.

At the very least, put up a home page, with basic information about your organization, a way for people to join you and/or subscribe to your e-newsletter, along with a way for people to get more information. You can flesh out the rest of the website over time, making it as rich and useful a resource for your community as possible.

Suggested Free Web Services

Weebly offers free website hosting and easy-to-use templates for designing and publishing websites. For more information, visit: www.weebly.com

Another free resource for website design, Joomla allows you to manage all of your own content in a simple way without effecting the major formatting of your website. For more information, visit: www.joomla.org

Keep Your Website Regularly Updated

Make sure to put all upcoming events, key meetings and important policy votes up on your website so people can easily check and have plenty of notice if they want to participate. Whenever possible, provide opportunities or suggestions for actions people can take either in their personal lifestyle or in the community to weigh in on local issues. Consider including a blog or twitter feed on your organization's current work or relevant events or issues in your community.

Use Social Media to Your Advantage

Social media gives you a quick and easy way to reach large audiences daily with fun, informative, useful information. Take advantage of it to communicate to and mobilize your subscribers.

Create your organization as a cause on Facebook, and use your page to spread the word about upcoming events and pertinent topics. This is an effective way to engage your subscribers in conversation and invite them to take action. You can include links to informative articles, share photos and videos, and encourage your supporters to share your posts on their walls.

Write a blog to report on events and offer relevant tips and topics, then find a local internet news site like the nationwide *Patch* (www.Patch.com) to pick up your blog and broadcast it to a larger audience.

Use Twitter to tweet instantly about relevent events in your area and share links to articles of interest.

Create a channel and post videos on YouTube. Cover topics of interest to your subscribers, such as rainwater harvesting, composting or other sustainable practices. Add more whenever you can.

The possibilities for using social media as an effective communication tool are endless and continue to grow. Growing with them will also help engage a younger audience to join your cause.

Stay in Touch with Your Subscriber List

Depending on how active your organization is and how much there is to report, send e-newsletters out to your subscriber list bi-weekly or monthly. But be sure to pick a schedule and stick to it.

Update your subscribers on your current work and upcoming events. To bulk up your newsletters a little, you can also include the events of other partner organizations to support their work, along with relevant local or global news. But keep your newsletter short and sweet, with links to your website for more detailed information.

Be Generous Hosts

Let your subscribers know about your upcoming events in a short email one week to one month in advance and then follow up with a reminder email a few days before the event. Ask other organizations doing related work to pass your invitation on to their subscribers.

Include Elected Officials and Other Key Players

No matter what the event is, always invite elected officials and other key players in your community to join you. This is an opportunity to make personal contact with them through a phone call or email. Remember to include your County Board of Supervisors, City Council, school board members, key city staff, members of public agencies and even Assemblymembers. Don't take it personally if they never show up, or stop inviting them in the future. It's always good for them to see your organization is vibrant and active.

Alert the Press

List your events in the community calendar section of your local newspapers and radio stations. Look for other online calendars of local events. Check on submission deadlines and contacts for each of your local press outlets. Keep a list of this information handy and be sure to update it as needed.

Always invite the local press to cover your events. Though reporters may rarely show up, work to develop personal relationships with them so they know who you are and what your organization represents. Send them a media alert prior to your event, then if they don't show up, follow up with a press release telling its story. Don't hesitate to contact them directly to gently correct any errors if they do write an article about you without your input.

As your organization builds credibility with local government and the community, reporters will begin to approach you for quotes, stories and perspectives for articles they are writing. Always respond to them as quickly and professionally as possible to maintain your relationship. *"It's an indicator of some success that [the newspapers] come to us for quotes."* says Ed Mainland of Sustainable Novato. *"They know that we're allied with [sustainability] initiatives, and we're right there, giving quotes and background to help them write their story."*

Helpful Hints:

Create a Media List for Easy Reference

Generate a list of reporters and assignment editors who might be interested in covering your cause. This will make your life easier each time you send out a media alert, press release or want to pitch a story. Your list should include at least one contact name, fax number, phone number, and e-mail address for each of your local newspapers, TV stations and radio news programs. Other organizations working on similar issues may share their list with you.

Keep track of all coverage your organization receives and be sure to thank reporters for good coverage.

Write and Send Media Alerts, Community Announcements, and Press Releases

Let the press know what you are up to in a variety of formats to ensure adequate coverage. It is always best to address a specific reporter or editor at each outlet and send to as many outlets as possible via fax or email. When emailing, never send attachments. Instead, copy and paste into the email message, ensuring there are no major formatting issues before sending. Be sure to include an exciting subject line to capture their attention. It is best to limit your items to one page.

Media Alert Standard Format

Media Alerts provide a brief snapshot of your event or story and just enough information to entice reporters to cover it. Send them twice- once two weeks prior to your event, and again two to three days before. They follow the sequence below:

- LOGO: Use your organization's logo and stationary if possible.
- MEDIA ALERT: Include the words "MEDIA ALERT" in the upper left corner, with the date you are sending it just below.
- CONTACT INFO: Skip a space and provide contact name, phone number and e-mail. Contacts listed should be prepared to be interviewed by reporters.
- HEADLINE/Subtitle: Center a catchy headline describing the event on the page. You can add a subtitle below this, which offers a little more information.
- WHAT: Catch their attention with a brief description, about a paragraph, of the purpose, or the *WHAT* of your event. Let reporters know what will take place, but don't provide so much information that they don't need to show up to cover it!
- WHO: List the speaker/s and their titles and/or who is sponsoring the event.
- WHY: Let them know why the event is being held.

- WHO SHOULD ATTEND: Who is the appropriate audience for the event?
- WHEN: List the date and time.
- WHERE: List the location of the event. Be specific so reporters will be able to find it!
- BONUS or VISUALS: List bonuses or photo opportunities, if any.
- CLOSING SYMBOL: Place the symbol: ### at the bottom center of the page. This is used to mark the end of the advisory so that reporters don't expect additional pages.

Press Release Standard Format:

Press Releases seek to capture the attention of a reporter or editor by telling the story of your event or other newsworthy item in the third person, and will at times be published word-for-word as you have written them. They follow the sequence below:

- LOGO: Use your organization's logo and stationary if possible.
- "FOR IMMEDIATE RELEASE": Include the words "FOR IMMEDIATE RELEASE" in the upper right corner of the page.
- CONTACT INFO: Provide contact name, phone numbers and e-mail for your organization in upper left corner of the page. Contacts listed should be prepared to be interviewed by reporters.

- HEADLINE/Subtitle: Center a catchy headline describing the event on the page. You can add a subtitle below this, which offers a little more information.

- PRESS RELEASE LEAD: The lead paragraph should include the who, what, where, when and how of the event.

- PRESS RELEASE BODY: This is where you provide more description and information. Include quotes and other supporting material to tell the story of your event or initiative. Remember, this can sometimes be published directly, so write it like a good article.

- BOILER PLATE: Describe your organization and what it does in one or two sentences. This is a standard text you will use each time you send a press release.

- FOLLOW UP: "If you would like more information on this topic, or to schedule an interview with [the contact person], please call [same or different contact person] or email [same or different contact person]."

- CLOSING SYMBOL: Place the symbol: ### at the bottom center of the page. This is used to mark the end of the advisory so that reporters don't expect additional pages.

Community Announcement Standard Format

Community Announcements and flyers provide a format that is easy to post around the community, list in the community calendar section of your local newspapers, or send off to other organizations to alert their constituencies.

- TITLE: Make it clear but catchy. One group titled an event focusing on waste *"Risk Management at the Redwood Landfill,"* and no one showed up for it. When they changed the title to: *"Where Will Our Trash Go?"* people showed up.

- SUBTITLE: Tell people why they need this information. It's a good place to ask a question they want the answer to.

- DATE, TIME, LOCATION, COURSE SPEAKER AND PRICE: Be very clear about whether you expect an RSVP or not.

- DESCRIPTION: Let them know what they will learn. Include links if you can.

- CONTACT INFORMATION: For more information.

- INVITATION: It is always nice to say something friendly and community building like *"Please join us,"* or *"We hope to see you there."*

Example: Media Alert

MEDIA ALERT

October 6, 2006

Contact: Pam Hartwell-Herrero • (415) --- ---- • ---@sustainablefairfax.org

Sustainable Backyard Series Continues

Natural Building with Cob

What: Sustainable Fairfax continues its educational offerings to the
community with this month's workshop, *Build a Garden Bench with Cob.*

Who: Sustainable Fairfax and Permaculture Experts

When: October 21 and 22, 10AM-4PM

Where: Sustainable Fairfax, 141 Bolinas Rd., Fairfax

Visuals: Photo opportunities of participants in action building cob garden
bench.

###

Example: Community Announcement

Interested in Reusing Your Greywater?
Hands-on Greywater Workshop

With drought, threats of rations and a proposed desalination plant, it is time we learn to recycle the water coming out of our showers, washing machines, and bathroom sinks. Want to learn more about it and how to build your own system? In this hands-on class we will take a top loading washing machine and route the rinse water into the nearby landscape.

Saturday, August 22nd from 11AM-4PM
Taught by Laura Allen of Greywater Action
Snacks and beverages will be provided. Bring your own lunch.

Cost: $40 to $100, sliding scale. Pay what you can, work-trade available. You must register! Space is limited.

For more information and to register go to www.sustainablefairfax.org or send a check to: Sustainable Fairfax, 141 Bolinas Rd., Fairfax, CA 94930

Please Join Us!

Example: Press Release

FOR IMMEDIATE RELEASE

CONTACT: Pam Hartwell-Herrero • (415) --- ---- • ---@sustainablefairfax.org

SUSTAINABLE BACKYARD SERIES CONTINUES
Sustainable Fairfax Announces Special Workshop in Natural Building

Fairfax, CA – October 10, 2006 – Sustainable Fairfax's Backyard Class series continues October 21-22, with a focus on natural building with cob. The cost is $100 for the weekend workshop.

Cob, a very old method of building using earth and straw or other fibers, was a common building material in England in the nineteenth century, and many buildings constructed with it at that time are still standing. It is similar to adobe, but instead of being formed into uniform blocks, cob is applied by hand in large gobs (or cobs) which can be tossed from one person to another during the building process. It is traditionally mixed with bare feet, as it is fairly labor intensive. Cob construction can be a wildly freeform, sculptural affair. In this two-day class participants will make a bench that will become a permanent piece of functional art in the Sustainable Backyard. Participants are encouraged to bring bits of tile, glass, ceramic and marbles to contribute to the bench. Sustainable Fairfax's Executive Director, Pam Hartwell-Herrero says, "it will be a fun, creative workshop with a beautiful result. for the community to enjoy."

Sustainable Fairfax began in February 1999 out of an inspiration to take local action on the global warming crisis. The Sustainable Backyard space will be a demonstration site for sustainable practices for outside the home. It will also be used for Sustainable Fairfax events and meetings and will be available for other local organizations to utilize.

For more information and to signup for the classes please contact, Pam Hartwell-Herrero at (415) --- ----, ---@sustainablefairfax.org.

###

Write Letters to the Editor and Op Ed Pieces

Submitting letters to the editor or writing Op Ed pieces is another way to bring attention to a sustainability initiative or call your community to action. Be sure to include well-researched information and consider how you are representing your organization as you write. Keep it credible and down to earth.

Brand Yourselves

Once your organization has reached a certain level of membership and visibility, if not before, you will want to develop a consistent look or 'brand' so people will recognize it in the community. Choose colors and design a logo, then consistently include them on all signs, brochures, websites, banners and items your organization produces. If there is not someone on your team who can donate these services, see if you can partner with a local graphic designer who will (and be sure to give them credit publicly if they do!).

Posters & Flyers

You will probably want to use as paperless an approach as possible in the interest of keeping costs low and saving natural resources. Still, there are times when a few well-placed and well-designed posters, flyers or signs can really help draw people to your event. Consider making a banner with your group name, logo and tagline out of a more durable material (i.e.; Tyvek) that can be used over and over again at events. Sandwich board signs can be made for individual events (plywood can be repainted over and over and weathers well).

Common Threads: Be In the Public Eye! ~ Getting the Word Out About Your Organization, Events & Initiatives

- Build a website and keep it updated.
- Keep up with social media as it evolves.
- Send newsletters to your email list.
- Invite elected officials, other non-profit organizations and beyond.
- Invite the press to all of your events and important policy meetings.
- Be available to give statements to reporters seeking a story.
- List your event in the 'Community Announcements' section of your local newspaper.
- Write letters to the editor and Op Ed pieces.
- Have a presence wherever there may be a media opportunity (i.e.; local parades and fairs, etc.).
- Design a logo and have consistent "brand" people will recognize.

CHAPTER SIX

The Value of Volunteers: Recruiting and Retaining Help

As your organization grows and in order to grow your organization, you'll need to put energy into recruiting new volunteers. The more volunteers you have, the lighter the workload and the less likelihood of burnout for your core members. The adage "many hands make light work" is all the more meaningful when it comes to a volunteer-run grassroots sustainability organization.

Here are a few ideas to help you attract and retain your volunteers.

Community Meetings and Events

Community meetings and events have great potential for recruiting new members and volunteers. Be sure your attendees sign in when they arrive and provide their contact information so you can send them your e-newsletter and keep them up to date on your work. Invite them to become members and/or volunteers during the event and in a follow up email thanking them for coming. Let them know the kinds of activities volunteers can engage in or the skills or services they could bring to the organization. If people simply want to join as members, let them know how their membership will benefit them and the organization, and that their financial contribution will go to good use.

"We find that community education is the best recruitment tool. People show up at our events; they like our events; they like what we're talking about; they like the people in the room; and they stay after and talk. We can barely get them out of the room when the event is over! We sign them up on our email subscriber list, which is now over a thousand. I would strongly recommend fun community education events that draw people in with [ideas and tips for] lifestyle changes and education, and then hone in on why you want to be making those lifestyle changes. We stay away from the doom and gloom, but we are very clear on positive solutions that you can be doing. That's a really good way to get people in."

Pam Hartwell-Herrero, Sustainable Fairfax

Co-Sponsor Events with Like-Minded Organizations

Co-sponsoring an event means sharing the workload as well as the proceeds, and gaining new audience members.

"In some of our early community education events, we found out what other people were doing and asked them to come do it for us. For example, SPAWN [the Salmon Protection And Watershed Network, www.spawnusa.org] does educational creek walks all winter, so we asked them if they'd do one just for us. We charge a fee and share proceeds and it's worked out really well. It's a great way to build relationships, educate ourselves and do some good networking. We didn't even plan to do it that way; we just wanted easy ways to do community education where we didn't have to work very hard because we didn't have very many volunteers at that point."

Pam Hartwell-Herrero, Sustainable Fairfax

Other examples include co-sponsoring a holiday recycled craft class with the Conservation Corps, a seed swap and garden exchange with a local Master Gardeners organization, or a talk on local food with a local co-op or grocer. Find your local sources of genius and tap into them.

Mine Interns and Volunteers from High Schools and Colleges

High Schools and colleges can be great resources for finding teens and young adults looking for opportunities to learn while contributing to their community. Consider this option if your organization has specific and meaningful projects or research that can be packaged for a young intern or volunteer. But also be aware that it requires time and energy to manage well. Interns often need a tailored program and want to learn and build their resume. It can take a lot of time to find a project that suits them, but it always pays off once you have them going on it.

Make sure you are prepared before taking on an intern and that you understand what they hope to get from the experience.

Offer Community Service Hours

Sign up with your County Probation office to be added as an organization with which people looking to fulfill community service hours can volunteer. This is a great way to rally more help during events.

Advertise on Your Website

Your website should always provide an opportunity for people to become volunteers or members, ideally with a secure option to make donations electronically. Make sure that someone from your organization follows up promptly with all new volunteers and members that come to you this way. You can set it up so that volunteer inquiries get forwarded directly to your volunteer coordinator and membership inquiries get forwarded directly to your membership coordinator.

Common Threads: Recruiting Members and Volunteers

- Have regular community meetings and/or events (at least monthly).
- Have sign-up sheets at all events inviting people to join mailing list or become members.
- Co-sponsor events with like-minded organizations.
- Consider working with young interns or volunteers.
- Provide an option to become members and/or volunteers on your website.

Working Well with Volunteers

"I just love that on a limited budget and with limited paid staff, we are able to accomplish so many things. I've been a volunteer my whole life and am incredibly warmed by people just giving their time. It's nice to work with people who are giving the best of themselves to make our community and our world a better place."

Pam Hartwell-Herrero, Sustainable Fairfax

Being a volunteer-run organization, you will want to put some thought into how you will work with new and ongoing volunteers to create an effective team with a high retention rate. A volunteer who is respected, empowered, valued, and given a chance to bring forth their particular gifts or talents is a satisfied volunteer who will stick around and invest his or her energy in the organization and its mission.

Plug New Volunteers in Efficiently

When people sign up to volunteer via your website or a sign-up sheet, follow up with contact immediately via phone or email. Find out what particular skills they have or what projects or initiatives interest them most, then funnel them to the appropriate committee chair to further the relationship and initiate them to the work. You may want to assign this task to a volunteer coordinator dedicated to working with new volunteers.

"Not everyone likes to do the same sorts of things. I've learned there are different types of volunteers and different ways in which they're looking to make a contribution or receive recognition. Some people are more than willing to take on essentially grunt labor and bang out the work, and others are looking to take a management position leading a group, planting the flag on the top of the hill and bringing others together."

John Schlag, Sustainable Novato

Ultimately, you want to invite your volunteers to take on some responsibility within the organization in a way that best serves their interests as well as those of the organization.

Educate Your Volunteers Properly

Your volunteers will be representing your organization and helping to spread the ripples of sustainability throughout your community. It is important to gauge their level of understanding of the principles of sustainability and your intitiatives, then provide them with appropriate education. Be sure to include a clear definition of the mission, structure and strategic initiatives of your organization. You can do this informally in conversation, or in a more structured way such as via a handbook or volunteer training workshop.

Case Study: Sustainable Fairfax Volunteer Core Training

Sustainable Fairfax offers a Volunteer Core Training once a year. This two-day training is designed so that volunteers become well-versed in the principles of sustainability and the organization's mission and strategic initiatives. It also covers the particulars of running the organization's Sustainability Center and leading tours of its permaculture demonstration garden. Local authors, such as Andres Edwards (*Sustainability Revolution*) or Warren Karlenzig (*How Green Is Your City?*), come in and give talks on sustainability which serve to inspire new volunteers.

All trained volunteers are required to staff one 4-hour shift at the Sustainability Center per month, as well as serve on a committee or start a project. *"Sometimes the Center is isolating because you're sitting there alone, or interacting with the community, but not really interacting with the organization,"* says Executive Director Pam Hartwell-Herrero. *"So we ask that every person join a committee so they get to know other people working in the organization and become involved in initiatives. We find that this really keeps people engaged."*

The number of participants ranges from eight to ten, and everyone is required to attend both days. If a new volunteer can't make the training they will still be invited to join a committee so as not to create any barriers to participating.

Sustainable Fairfax offers a number of different levels of participation and responsibility to their volunteers, including:

- seats on their board or committees
- participation in the Volunteer Corps
- project leadership
- participation as Community Volunteers (people who occasionally help out on small projects, i.e.; weeding the demonstration garden, helping at events)

Sustainable Fairfax has also developed a more in-depth Sustainability Corps certificate. Volunteers receive this certificate once they've staffed a certain number of hours at the Center and participated in a committee or project. This higher level certificate encourages volunteers to build a more engaging, ongoing relationship with the organization, and is a great resume builder.

Example: Volunteer Core Training Homework Assignment

One of the things we'll be discussing at the training is the future of Fairfax, and our role in creating it. To facilitate and inspire this exploration, we're asking participants to give some advance thought to this topic, in the form of a homework assignment (don't panic, it's fun!).

Please write a brief story, poem or letter titled "Fairfax in the Year 2050". Let the following questions inspire you as you think and write:

- Do you feel optimistic or pessimistic?
- What are your main hopes?
- What are your primary fears?
- What do you wish for more than anything?
- Describe the town that you want for your children and their children…

Have fun with this! It's a golden opportunity to organize and articulate your thoughts and feelings about the big picture.

Some excerpts from one participant's response:

"[My vision of Fairfax is]…as a vibrant social and cultural center where people are brought together through respect for and deep understanding of the natural environment and community that supports them.

Land use is transformed back into the lifeblood of economic, social, and cultural meaning, as an expression of this integrated relationship. As the human connection to the land as a source of subsistence is reawakened, the pace of life slows down to mimic natural cycles and geological processes, proceeding deliberately as part of an integral web of interconnectedness. The costs of living decrease as the quality of life increases due to a combination of more essential needs being grown and processed locally and our consumptive materialistic tendencies being replaced by the satisfaction that comes with deep meaningful relationships with people and place.

To support these transitions, public officials become more responsive and inclusive of the opinions and desires of the general populace while businesses help to contribute to re-engineering the infrastructure to support this community. Educational programs are shifted towards a mentorship model, providing skills and perspective that reflect changing needs while portraying big picture systems-based approaches to living. The concept of waste is eliminated from our vocabulary and each individual is empowered and encouraged to be a responsible steward with a high level of influence over how their needs are met and the overall quality of life for all."

-Jeffrey Adams, Volunteer

Example: Sustainable Fairfax Volunteer Community Service Project Form

Thanks for your interest in starting a Community Service Project! Part of Sustainable Fairfax's mission is to serve the community through projects such as the creation of the Downtown Fairfax Recycling Bins, Green Wednesdays or perhaps a Sustainability Book Club. These projects are a way for our volunteers to be active in bettering our community and meeting its diverse needs.

Your project must be grounded in the Mission of Sustainable Fairfax. It must benefit a sustainable practice or policy in one or more of our target areas:

- Local economy and community self-reliance
- Environmental preservation or regeneration
- Community building

Your project must be with and for Sustainable Fairfax or another non-profit organization, community group, school, town or government agency within our sphere of influence. Projects may be initiated by a group or by a single volunteer. Sustainable Fairfax volunteers must collaborate with others on organizing and executing the project.

Sustainable Fairfax volunteers choose the projects they give their time to, therefore, Sustainable Fairfax cannot guarantee assistance by other volunteers, but will try to help if a volunteer backs out. In the event of your departure as a volunteer, we ask that you seek to engage a replacement to take over responsibility for the continuation or maintenance of your project.

Example: Sustainable Fairfax Project Information

Project name _____

Project Location _____

Project duration or date _____

SFx Volunteer Contact _____

Organization working with SFx _____

Contact at other organization _____

Description of project _____

_____

_____

_____

How does this project fit our Mission? _____

_____

_____

What are the SFx resources requested ?_____

_____

Is there any chance this will bring in donations for SFx?_____

_____

_____

Please submit form to Pam Hartwell-Herrero ---@sustainablefairfax.org or to
Project Chair.

Give Volunteers Ownership

Encourage your volunteers to share their ideas, take the lead on projects and initiate collaborations. Look for ways to engage them without overly directing them so that they feel pride and ownership in their contribution.

"When I started out with Sustainable Fairfax, the founder told me, 'Pam, you can do this.' That empowerment was a real gift to me, and I try to give that gift as often as I possibly can. I meet volunteers who say, 'I don't know what I have to offer,' and I help them find something and make them feel really good about it. Because it felt so good to me and that's nice to do for people."

Pam Hartwell-Herrero, Sustainable Fairfax

Honor Your Volunteers

Besides casually expressing gratitude and appreciation for people's contributions, it is a good practice to periodically recognize the work of your volunteers in some more formal way. Recognition might be via annual certificates or awards, or posting the "volunteer of the month or season" on your website. If working with high school students on campus or community-wide sustainability projects, this kind of recognition can be an excellent addition to their college application files.

Expect Waxing and Waning Participation

"Sometimes a bright star will suddenly give you a lot of energy and talent, and then something happens in their family or business and they're not there any more. That's just a fact of life with non-profits."

Ed Mainland, Sustainable Novato

Be prepared for volunteers to come and go, and give varying levels of energy and time. Because, like you, they are contributing their time for free, your organization and its work may take the back seat to other obligations at times. Try to be gracious, understanding and flexible about this.

Letting a Volunteer Go

Sometimes a volunteer just isn't a good fit for your organization. There can be instances where someone is clearly looking to use the organization for their personal gain, or to promote their business. It is important to let them know that while you appreciate their service, you want their first priority while volunteering to be to the organization. If it continues to be a problem, bring it to the attention of the board, and with the board's approval, you can let the volunteer go.

Another common challenge can be a volunteer committing to do things, then dropping the ball and not following through. This can be a big problem if they are a board member or lead project coordinator. Always do what is best for the organization and let them go if you are unable to inspire them to bring more of themselves to the work. In this case, it is best to have a frank discussion during which you can say something along the lines of: *"I know your heart is in the right place but it doesn't seem you have the time to really give what you want to give right now."* Giving them an out is always nicer than asking them to leave.

A similar conversation can be had with a volunteer who consistently complains or expresses a negative attitude. Such an attitude can be toxic and spread to other volunteers and it is best to head this off as early as possible.

Handling Conflict

Sustainable Fairfax includes the document on the following pages in its new volunteer packet to prevent the kinds of issues listed above and others, and provide support if they do arise.

Example: Sustainable Fairfax Conflict Management

All Sustainable Fairfax volunteers agree to:
Create and maintain a positive experience for everyone.
Bring our best work to the organization.
Present a united organization to community.
Create consistent policies throughout the organization.

Two kinds of conflict that have challenged us in the past:
Charged organizational decisions.
Interpersonal issues.

To prevent organizational conflict Sustainable Fairfax volunteers agree that:
We are all here for the good of the organization.
We are not here to use the organization for political or financial gain.
Meetings will have agendas with pre–determined items.
Topics for discussion will be given to the facilitator in advance.
Facilitator will give notice about agenda items to all participants.
We will use the 'gradients of agreement' tool for difficult decisions.
Reaching consensus and making sure everyone is heard is a priority, and may take more than one meeting.

Steps to handle conflict and interpersonal issues:
- Keep meetings focused on the business of the organization.
- Contact someone on Executive Board for help.
- During a meeting, the facilitator will decide how to handle conflict:

    In this meeting   Outside of meeting
    Next meeting   Special meeting   Mediation

Example: Sustainable Fairfax Conflict Management
(continued)

Confidentiality Policy: All Sustainable Fairfax volunteers understand that we:
Talk about our work with people outside the organization.
Answer people's questions about the board and organization.
Learn by discussing our work with other non-profit people or professional confidants.

We need to use common sense & be professional: Our organization depends on funding and support from the local community, its citizens and businesses.
 It is best for the organization when:

- We preserve anonymity on interpersonal issues.

- One just needs to vent that he or she do it in a safe place with a safe person who will protect the reputation & standing of Sustainable Fairfax.

- Projects that have not gone public yet are kept confidential. Keep yourself informed on project status.

- Dealing with local government, potential funders and the press to refer an inquisitive person to our President, Executive Director or the lead person on a project.

Common Threads: The Value of Volunteers ~ Recruiting and Retaining Help

- Don't let your volunteers slip through the cracks.

- Have a volunteer coordinator dedicated to assigning volunteers appropriate roles, teams and tasks.

- Find out what their interests are and plug them in appropriately.

- Educate your volunteers on the principles of sustainability, your mission, your strategic initiatives.

- Empower your volunteers.

- Recognize and honor their work.

- Be flexible if they wax and wane. They are volunteering their time, after all.

- Be prepared to address potential conflict in a powerful manner.

- Let go of volunteers who are toxic to the cause.

CHAPTER SEVEN

What Will it Cost Us? Funding Your Work

"We were able to do a lot considering we had no money, a small group of people, and not that much time commitment, either. We were all working full time, and didn't have a lot of time to work on this. It's just another example of what people can do regardless of financial resources."

Marie Kerpan, Sustainable Mill Valley

It is possible to keep your costs extremely low if you aren't paying for a dedicated office or staff to run your organization. Gathering in people's living rooms, attending City Council meetings and meeting with other stakeholders doesn't require any money, just time.

But as your work and visibility expand, so may your costs. Things such as website development, hosting and maintenance, printing of flyers, brochures, banners and signs, materials and refreshments for meetings, or venue rental and insurance will start to crop up and demand funding.

Securing financial support can help your organization increase its capacity and effectiveness. Finding a way to hire paid staff in the form of a Program Assistant or Executive Director can be of great benefit to the organization. As it grows, you may find someone in a leadership role who is willing to raise the money needed to pay themselves on a part-time basis. This paid staff person can bring continuity to your organization, and dedication to keeing it vibrant and strong.

Fiscal Sponsorship vs. Non-Profit Status

If you are going to be soliciting donations or grants, paying people salaries or opening a bank account, you will need to either incorporate your organization as a 501(c)(3) non-profit, or find an established non-profit organization whose mission relates strongly to yours and ask them to act as your fiscal sponsor. Sustainable Marin acts as the fiscal sponsor for most of the sustainable town and city organizations featured in this guide.

A fiscal sponsor shares its legal and tax-exempt status as well as some administrative services in exchange for an administrative fee that typically ranges from five to ten percent of all monies raised by your organization. It accepts financial and legal liability for your organization, and lends its credibility to yours, thereby increasing potential for securing grants. A fiscal sponsor will often also manage grant monies and provide liability insurance for venue rental. All of this can be worth the administrative fee if your group does not have the time or money to go through the process of incorporating as a non-profit. But having a fiscal sponsor also means that your organization will lose some autonomy. Your fiscal sponsor will have to approve your organization's strategic initiatives and actions. If your missions are aligned, this should not be too difficult.

If you decide to incorporate as a non-profit, there are many resources available online to guide you through the process. You will be able to do much of the work yourselves, but would be wise to seek some guidance from a lawyer who is familiar with this process.

Funding Resources

Whatever your funding needs are, there are many ways to raise funds. Consider appointing a Funding Development Chair to look for potential grants and other funding opportunities, such as:

Membership Contributions

As your organization gains visibility, credibility and respect for the work it does locally, community members will become more and more willing to support its efforts with annual membership contributions. Consider keeping your dues very modest; for example, thirty dollars for individuals, fifty dollars for households and one hundred dollars for businesses. New members should be welcomed at any time, and once a year you should run a membership renewal campaign. Ask local businesses to donate coupons you can offer with new memberships. This will generate new members for your organization, and direct people to patronize these businesses. This is also a great way to funnel people in to supporting local businesses. Sustainable Fairfax enjoys their biggest month of new membership each August when they offer coupons for free ice cream through their partnership with the local organic ice cream shop.

Donations

You may also ask for suggested donations when offering a talk, class, tour or workshop. Again, consider keeping the amount on the low side so as not to exclude anyone, for example, five to ten dollars for a two-hour talk, fifteen dollars for a tour, and thirty-five dollars or more for a three-hour workshop. It is good to keep your class prices affordable and not turn people away for lack of funds. It is also nice to be able to pay your speakers or workshop leaders an honorarium from the donations collected.

Large Donors

Large donors are those who contribute between $500.00 and $5,000.00 or more. In most communities there are wealthy people who like to support good causes. Find these people by asking around your community. Perhaps your local elected officials will share the names of donors who made large contributions to their campaigns. Get an introduction through a mutual friend, strike up a conversation about the work you are doing, or invite them to an event that you are hosting. If they seem interested, ask them for a specific amount just above what you think they might give and be sure to let them know that it is support from people like them that makes your work possible. Remember to follow up with a thank you note and ask if they will allow more public acknowledgement. If so, mention them at big events and on your website. Doing so may encourage others to make generous contributions. And remember to ask your large donors to contribute generously each year.

In-Kind Donations and Sponsorships from Local Businesses

Don't be afraid to ask for other types of donations. Look to partner with local businesses that might donate services, venues for events or meetings, printing, food, drink or anything else your organization might need. Make sure to hold up your end of the bargain by consistently letting your membership know who your business partners and sponsors are and encouraging them to shop locally.

Often there are local skilled workers who want to reach your audience by helping you with a class that is related to the work they do. They will get some good advertising and you will get a free speaker or some skilled work done. Businesses may also be willing to give cash donations to sponsor your work. In return you can feature them on your website or in your newsletter.

"I think that businesses see that if they connect with us they get a good little bump of cache. They occasionally donate money or sponsor an event, and in return we send them customers and educate people on why they should be shopping locally."

Pam Hartwell-Herrero, Sustainable Fairfax

It Pays To Be Connected

You're more likely to get funding if you know someone within the organization, foundation or business from which you seek it. Or if you know someone who knows someone… It's just the way it is. Find people to serve on your board who are well connected in the community.

Grants: Local Government

Many cities and counties have small amounts of discretionary funding available in their budgets to support local action. They are often happy when community organizations take on projects that would cost them much more to tackle themselves. Sustainable Fairfax receives more regular funding from the County of Marin than from any other source.

Maintaining positive relationships with local elected officials can also help when it comes time to procure letters of recommendation for other grants you may be seeking. These officials may also be able to share valuable connections that can lead to other grants or funding sources.

Grants: Foundations

There are many foundations that fund sustainability work, and their board members are often required to disburse a certain number of grants per funding cycle. Knowing the right people can make or break your funding request. Ask everyone you know whether they serve on the board of a foundation or know someone who does. Network and make the important connections you'll need to get funded.

"We started finding smaller, family foundation grants through people we knew. It's amazing how networking works!"

Pam Hartwell-Herrero, Sustainable Fairfax

Fundraising Parties

Fundraising parties are a celebratory efficient way to bring in funds. Consider providing some sort of entertainment, such as live music or a compelling speaker to draw people in. Seek partnerships with local businesses that will donate items or services for silent auctions, food and beverage for attendees, décor or a venue for the party. Charge more than you would for an educational event (it is a fundraiser, after all) and invite widely.

Common Threads: What Will It Cost Us? ~ Funding Your Work

- If you're going to need funds, incorporate as a non-profit or seek a fiscal sponsor.

- Run regular membership campaigns, and partner with local businesses to offer new members incentives.

- Ask for donations at all of your events.

- Look for large donors in your community.

- Approach local businesses for in-kind donations, and be sure to acknowledge those that do contribute on your website and at your events.

- Network and use your connections to lead you to potential funders.

- Throw parties!

CHAPTER EIGHT

Other Things to Consider

Doing the noble work of building sustainability into your community, while rewarding, is not without its challenges and setbacks. But don't let that stop you. Knowing what you might expect and planning appropriately will save you a lot of time, energy and frustration in the long run.

Be Patient: Change Takes Time

It's just a fact of life that effecting important change in local government, school districts and the community takes time and requires an inordinate amount of patience.

"It always takes much more time than we would like to create change. I wish with all my heart that we had a city and a school district where sustainability was a core value and from the ground up it was how we lived and breathed, but we're not there yet. But I think, thanks to [our core] people, other incredible people and all the volunteers we have, we're really starting to turn the battle ship around. But it takes a lot."

Annan Paterson, Sustainable Novato

Tackle Outdated Paradigms, Old Mindsets and Budget Limitations

"I still see that there really isn't a connect-the-dots mentality in terms of how the environment, the economy, and humans can work in harmony."

Annan Paterson, Sustainable Novato

Now and again, you may find yourselves running up against what you perceive to be outdated paradigms and old mindsets that view the environment, community well-being and the economy as mutually exclusive. You will likely encounter arguments and roadblocks centered around budget and staff limitations, and school boards and City Councils may regularly or perpetually want to put real sustainability concerns on the back burner in order to deal with their bottom line.

While budget and staff limitations are legitimate concerns and should be taken seriously, innovative solutions can often be found through partnerships and creative thinking. Offer to work collaboratively with school board or City Council members to find solutions and implement them. Get children or teens involved, as they often inspire leaders to find their way to a yes vote. Your leadership, as well as your patience and persistence will help to change minds and shift paradigms over time.

"This is a chief obstacle, the economic tsunami that has hit us, because it's very convenient for politicians to say, 'we don't have the money for all this "green" stuff.' What we're preaching, though, is actually how to save them money, save them energy and save them resources, and show them how in the long run they'll be better off. Unless you can be competent and persuasive with numbers, the City Council won't even give you the time of day."

Ed Mainland, Sustainable Novato

Persist in the Face of Disappointment, Resistance and Failed Initiatives

No matter how disappointing or devastating a setback or failed initiative is, you must not give up or let your anger get the better of you. Keep the long-term, larger focus of creating a sustainable community in mind when you feel defeated. Continue your efforts to educate and change minds, and keep working on recruiting people to your cause.

"When [we first started,] the City Council sort of looked down their nose at people. I was shocked when I first went to meetings and saw how the public was treated. We knew it wasn't going to be a cakewalk, but I guess we were surprised at some of the resistance and attitude of the Council. It was hard to be taken seriously. But you know, in time it's like water on a rock. You just wear away on the rock. You keep showing up and writing letters and making suggestions and bringing in more people. We have a really responsive Council now."

Marie Kerpan, Sustainable Mill Valley

(In response to the Novato City Council not passing the Marin Clean Energy measure:)

"You can't afford to roll over and let it go. You have to be persistent as long as there is any hope of changing the minds of any City Council. We have a few months [and another chance] left. We have to find another angel on City Council in order to effect any change in their position…"

Marie Chan, Sustainable Novato

Avoid Burnout

"The burnout factor is there, and the way to address it is to identify chunks that you can put a bow on and hand to someone else. But there is also juice. We feel like we're making a bit of a difference, and we really

have an opportunity to be with like-minded others. We have lovely people who come to our meetings. It's really like being with family in a way."

Kiki LaPorta, Sustainable San Rafael

Burnout can definitely be a side-effect of doing grassroots volunteer work. Feeling passionate about an issue and knowing its urgency will sometimes lead you to get in over your head. Before you know it, things in your personal and professional life are being neglected and your stress level has increased. Take care to monitor yourself along the way and try to create some kind of balance or harmony. If you talk to long-time activists or organizers in your community and ask them how they have kept at it for so long, they will often say: 'Pace yourself, have support both within the organization and outside with family and friends, and do what truly inspires you.'

Build Your Capacity & Share the Workload

When a small core group of active volunteers is doing all of the work on top of their professional and personal lives, they will often forget to prioritize putting time and energy into recruiting new volunteers. But advancing sustainability initiatives in your city takes commitment and persistence, and recruiting new volunteers

to share the workload will help sustain your organization and its success over time. It is well worth the time and effort it takes.

"It's a trajectory." Says Marie Kerpan. "You do something for a while, you have a lot of energy for it, and then if you don't get reinforcements and the thing doesn't grow in a particular way, there is just a natural evolution of losing steam."

Monitor Your Energy and Pace Yourselves

Sometimes despite your best efforts to recruit, you may have periods of difficulty drawing people in. In this case, consider how else you might sustain the work of your organization. Monitor your energy and keep a realistic pace that works for you. Make adjustments in your level of participation that allow you to sustain yourself and your focus in the organization over time. Consider scaling back on an initiative if it will protect the organization's longevity. Take time off to evaluate what is really important to you, then come back and focus on that.

Find What's "Juicy" for You and Do It!

When you first get involved with the organization, take your time getting to know its core members, its mission and strategic initiatives. Read up on the principles of sustainability, meet members of your City Council, school board, local business and non-profit community and planning commission. Zero in on the particular aspects and interests that are engaging and appropriate for you, then try to focus your work on them.

Have Fun!

Finally, it is important to remember to have fun! While much of your work as an organization will focus on serious business, how you approach it will make all the difference.

"I think one of the reasons people like to be around us is because even though we are totally and completely aware that our work is grounded in a horrible sense of loss, we are able to see the bright side of it and we're determined to have a good time making the world a better place. There are definitely tears and moments of fear and challenge, but we know that we have to be doing something and we might as well have a good time doing it."

Pam Hartwell-Herrero, Sustainable Fairfax

Common Threads: Other Things To Consider

- Change takes time. Be patient and trust that your efforts will have effect in the long-run.

- Use creative thinking and partnerships to address perceived and actual limitations of budget and staff time.

- Demonstrate the cost-benefit of an initiative that is meeting resistance.

- Don't let setbacks or losses get you down. Keep your long-term vision in mind and be persistent.

- Build your capacity and spread out the workload.

- Reflect on how much you can take on and still maintain harmony or balance.

- Know when to say 'no.'

- Keep a pace that is realistic for you.

- Delegate pieces of the work to others. Don't do it all yourself.

- Build in and/or allow for variety if possible.

- Focus on the aspects of the organization and the work that give you juice.

- Look for ways to have fun doing the work!

Begin

Your community is a microcosm of the world, and a perfect place to start effecting the change you want to see in it.

The examples of community organizing provided in this guidebook are representative of the generosity and commitment of a collective of people who have offered their heart, time, vision and energy to their respective communities.

How will you use your own vision and energy to lead your community towards becoming more thriving and sustainable? What will you contribute to the growing conversation and practices prizing environmental, social and economic justice, well-being and integration?

There are a thousand and one ways, but don't let that overwhelm you. Just begin. Let yourself be drawn forward by the elements that most inspire and fill you with energy and hope. Find your friends, find your allies, find your partners, and go to work.

Case Studies: Advocating for Sustainable Policy

"It is a painstakingly slow process; all the initiatives that we are involved in require a tremendous amount of patience and persistence."

Marie Chan, Sustainable Novato

Case Study: Community Choice Law, Sustainable Fairfax:

When Sustainable Fairfax was founded in 1999, the most pressing issue at the time was how to address climate change at a local level because the upper level government was doing little at best, and tremendous damage at worst. Sustainable Fairfax founder, Rebekah Collins, had learned that electricity generation was responsible for nearly 50% of all greenhouse gas emissions. As she was researching the issue, she found that Community Choice Law offered some excellent solutions to help municipalities greatly reduce emissions.

The law had been applied in Massachusetts to allow municipalities to bypass their local utility and create a public/private hybrid utility. The new public utility could purchase electricity from the existing private utility while still using its distribution lines and customer service. This provided an opportunity for the public entity to choose a cleaner mix with more renewable energy without taking on the burden of service, distribution, and shareholder profit margins and still keep rates competitive. This arrangement also allowed the public entity to direct profits made in the purchase agreements to the community in the form of energy efficiency programs and local power building.

Rebekah led Sustainable Fairfax in holding public forums on the possibility of implementing the Community Choice Law locally, and invited all the elected officials in the County to attend. The Fairfax Town Council signed on to Cities for Climate Protection (CCP) Campaign through the International Council for Local Environmental Initiatives (ICLEI). Through the CCP Campaign, city governments join other city governments in signing an agreement to reduce greenhouse gas emissions in their city.

Members of the Fairfax Town Council began to urge County officials to champion the Community Choice Law. County Supervisor Hal Brown was the first to agree, and some time after, the County funded part of a feasibility study, with the Marin Municipal Water District, the largest electricity

International Council for Local Environmental Initiatives

ICLEI (www.iclei.org) is an international association of local governments as well as national and regional local government organizations that have made a commitment to sustainable development. ICLEI provides technical consulting, training, and information services to build capacity, share knowledge, and support local government in the implementation of sustainable development at the local level. ICLEI's basic premise is that locally designed initiatives can provide an effective and cost-efficient way to achieve local, national, and global sustainability objectives.

user in the county, funding the remaining portion. The study found the Community Choice Law to be a great deal.

Now, after several years of herculean work and leadership by many local allied elected officials, organizations and individuals, Marin Clean Energy is a reality run by County elected officials and known as the Marin Energy Authority (MEA). One by one, each city in the county has joined the MEA, and ratepayers can now purchase Marin Clean Energy's cleaner, more renewable energy portfolio, including a "deep green" option of 100% renewable power.

Sustainable Fairfax's initial work on this campaign inspired and helped pave the way for these other cities, and now neighboring counties are looking to join as well.

Case Study: Cities for Climate Protection Campaign, Sustainable Novato & Sustainable San Rafael:

Sustainable Novato's first strategic initiatives were climate change and greenhouse gas emissions reduction. *"At that time,"* founding and current board member Ed Mainland says, *"it was already obvious that our present course was not only unsustainable but also imminently catastrophic."*

In January 2003, members of Sustainable Novato introduced the CCP Campaign to a member of their City Council who had a "fairly green" track record. He immediately saw the campaign's merit and took the reins, introducing a resolution to the City Council and getting it passed.

Unfortunately, due to extreme budget constraints since the City Council adopted the CCP campaign, progress has been slow for the city of Novato.

Similar budget constraints initially kept the City of San Rafael from adopting the CCP Campaign when members of Sustainable San Rafael first introduced it. But Sustainable San Rafael members were not prepared to give up. They went back to the drawing board, and in their research discovered the US Conference of Mayors Climate Protection Agreement (www.usmayors.org/climateprotection/agreement.htm). This "taking it into your hands version of the Kyoto Protocol" was initiated by Mayor Nichols of Seattle, and as of late 2011, 1054 mayors from the fifty states, the District of Columbia and Puerto Rico, have signed the agreement, representing a total population of over 88,499,854 citizens.

Sustainable San Rafael went directly to the mayor armed with books and articles on climate change and asked him on the record to sign the agreement. Eventually he did. *"That was kind of the springboard."* said Kiki LaPorta, then president of Sustainable San Rafael. *"It was the first stake in the ground in terms of making putting attention on greenhouse gas reduction real."*

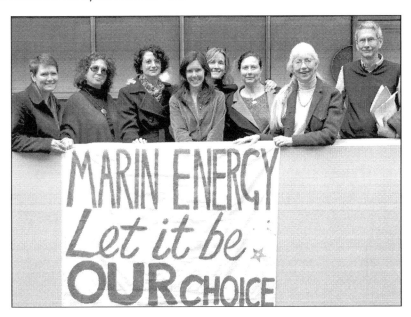

Before the city of San Rafael could take any meaningful action to study and reduce city greenhouse gas emissions, it needed to pass a measure increasing city sales tax in order to continue to fund basic city services. In the spirit of collaboration, members of Sustainable San Rafael committed to help pass the measure, promising that once it had passed, they would be back to push the issue of city greenhouse gas reductions. The voters approved the sales tax measure,

You can view San Rafael's CCAP at: www.cityofsanrafael.org/Government/ Community_Development/Green_ Initiatives/Documents

Provide Materials to Support Your Case

Provide well-researched, accessible materials to key players prior to important meetings so that they have a chance to review the information.

The Cities for Climate Protection™ (CCP) Campaign

The CCP Campaign (www.iclei.org/index. php?id=10829) assists cities to adopt policies and implement quantifiable measures to reduce local greenhouse gas emissions, improve air quality, and enhance urban livability and sustainability. More than 700 local governments participate in the CCP, integrating climate change mitigation into their decision-making processes. The CCP Campaign provides a structure and resources to help cities achieve five milestones in reducing their greenhouse gas emissions.

and at last the City Council passed a resolution to undertake the Cities for Climate Protection Campaign. Following this resolution, the mayor established a Green Ribbon Committee and Green Teams to develop the Climate Change Action Plan (CCAP) for the city of San Rafael. Members of Sustainable San Rafael sit on the committee and teams, and have been intimately involved in the development of the CCAP.

Cities for Climate Protection™ (CCP) Campaign Milestones

Milestone 1. Conduct a baseline emissions inventory and forecast. Based on energy consumption and waste generation, the city calculates greenhouse gas emissions for a base year (i.e.; 2000) and for a forecast year (i.e.; 2015). The inventory and forecast provide a benchmark against which the city can measure progress.

Milestone 2. Adopt an emissions reduction target for the forecast year. The city establishes an emission reduction target. The target both fosters political will and creates a framework to guide the planning and implementation of measures.

Milestone 3. Develop a Local Action Plan. Through a multi-stakeholder process, the city develops a Local Action Plan that describes the policies and measures that the local government will take to reduce greenhouse gas emissions and achieve its emissions reduction target. Most plans include a timeline, a description of financing mechanisms, and an assignment of responsibility to departments and staff. In addition to direct greenhouse gas reduction measures, most plans also incorporate public awareness and education efforts.

Milestone 4. Implement policies and measures. The city implements the policies and measures contained in their Local Action Plan. Typical policies and measures implemented by CCP participants include energy efficiency improvements to municipal buildings and water treatment facilities, streetlight retrofits, public transit improvements, installation of renewable power applications, and methane recovery from waste management.

Milestone 5. Monitor and verify results. Monitoring and verifying progress on the implementation of measures to reduce or avoid greenhouse gas emissions is an ongoing process. Monitoring begins once measures are implemented and continues for the life of the measures, providing important feedback that can be used to improve the measures over time.

Case Study: Green Schools Coalition, Sustainable Novato

The idea of "greening" local schools was proposed at one of Sustainable Novato's early general meetings. At the time, this concept was not well-understood among the fourteen schools within the Novato Unified School District (NUSD), and budget limitations were likely to keep it that way.

Besides being the largest public school district in Marin County, serving eight thousand children, NUSD also has the greatest budgetary challenges, receiving the lowest per capita funding in the county, while other districts receive as much as three times the per student funding.

Sustainable Novato committed to support the school district, and designated 'Green Schools' as one of its first strategic initiatives. *"We wanted to share our resources and knowledge base, and develop a voice so that we could engage the school district and help move the Green Schools cause forward,"* explains Marie Chan, Sustainable Novato's Vice President of Environmental Health. With this, they established a Green Schools Committee, the goal of which was to organize a group effort within the district and develop a framework for sustainability. *"We started with a round table and invited representatives from all the schools. Out*

of that we then formed what's called 'the Green Schools Coalition.'" The coalition was populated with members of Sustainable Novato, students, teachers and other community members. Through a series of five well-conceived meetings, the Green Schools Coalition established its mission statement, vision statement and charter.

Once the Green Schools Coalition was focused and organized, it invited the district board to collaborate. The board agreed to form a standing Sustainability Committee to advise the district on Indoor Air Quality, Integrated Pest Management, recycling and organic gardens as teaching tools. The Committee would to be populated with representatives from the Green Schools Coalition.

No sooner had the Committee formed than it was faced with an enormous challenge: the school district, which for years had benefited from free trash removal, would now be charged $250,000 for the service. This unbudgeted amount represented a huge hardship for the already struggling school district.

"[This was] a great motivator, and the timing was just perfect for the Green Schools Coalition," continues Marie, *"We had already formed. We were already organized. We were the only group that was ready on the ground with volunteers in all the schools, ready to implement. So the partnership*

was kind of [formed] out of need. We were going to be able to help the district solve the problem of this $250,000 bill."

The Green Schools Coalition saw that implementing a recycling program could help foot some of the bill, with California Refund Values (CRV) paying for recycled bottles and cans. They knew they could help organize a massive recycling effort throughout the district, and that every pound of cans and bottles diverted from trash cans to recycling bins would reduce the district's trash disposal bill. NUSD proposed this idea in a meeting with Novato's waste hauler, North Bay Corps, and was able to negotiate a more manageable bill.

Until this point, recycling in the district had been spotty, occurring on only a few of the thirteen campuses and run by a handful of volunteers. The Green Schools Coalition made this its primary focus in its first year. Over the next several years, all of the schools in the district received waste audits, as well as free recycling bins from the Conservation Corps of the North Bay (CCNB)- formerly the Conservation Corps of Marin. Now, a very focused recycling effort is being carried out throughout the district, with students leading the charge.

"Through well-developed partnerships that the Green Schools Coalition built along the way, we now have a memorandum of agreement between NUSD and the Conservation Corps of the North Bay, who have partnered to empty the recycling bins at no cost to our school district," Marie Chan reports, "Beyond this, Novato Disposal has also partnered with NUSD to further reduce trash disposal cost by encouraging the establishment of full-scale food composting at the Lynwood Central kitchen and organic garden as well as other organic school garden sites."

Unfortunately, the future of the Sustainability Committee is now in jeopardy due to budget cuts that have eliminated NUSD's Executive Director of Facilities, who has served as the committee's Co-Chair.

Green Schools Coalition of Novato Charter

OUR VISION:
The Green Schools Coalition of Novato envisions a healthy, sustainable school environment,

- that is free of toxins,
- that nourishes our students well in a green, healthy space,
- that effectively engages students in all aspects of their education, including environmental education,
- that uses resources sustainably.

OUR MISSION:
The mission of the Coalition is to advocate and support effective, safe, and sustainable practices throughout the Novato Unified School District.

OUR MAIN ROLES:
The Coalition will act as sustainability educators, resource-builders, and collaborative leaders.

OUR KEY STAKEHOLDERS:
The Coalition recognizes that our three key stakeholders are the students, the parents/ guardians, and the Novato Unified School District itself.

PROCEDURES *(a sampling)*:
- Only schools have a vote, and 1 school = 1 vote.
- To qualify as a voting member, a school must send a representative to the meetings at least part of the time. Even if a school cannot actively participate, it will still reap the benefits of our programs.
- As we are bound to the school district and primarily to the school principals, the Green Schools Coalition of Novato is an advocacy and advisory group to the NUSD. We work in collaboration with the school principals and other District staff.
- Partner organizations would be NON-VOTING members. The current partners are Sustainable Novato, Novato Live Well Network, Marin Conservation Corps, and the Indoor Air Quality (IAQ) Steering Committee.

Case Study: Green Building Ordinance, Sustainable San Rafael

Since buildings are one of the largest contributors of greenhouse gasses in a city, Sustainable San Rafael wanted the city to adopt a robust residential green building ordinance as an element of its Climate Change Action Plan. They set to work researching green ordinances already in place in other cities, and put together a Green Building Team, which included two City Council members and a member of the City Planning Commission, to discuss the process of writing and passing such an ordinance for San Rafael.

"We started out by meeting several times to educate ourselves and get impassioned on why we wanted [a green building ordinance], what it was going to do for greenhouse gas reduction, what it was going to do for the community, and why green building was a good thing for sustainability."

Kiki LaPorta, Sustainable San Rafael

They sought out experts, knowing that their input would boost the initiative's credibility. This networking led them to the director of Build It Green and other leaders in the field of green building through Stop Waste, a progressive agency in neighboring Alameda County.

Once they had done their homework, Sustainable San Rafael members held a study session with their City Council to bring them up to speed. The City Council directed its Community Development Director to develop the ordinance and Sustainable San Rafael plied him with research, sample ordinances from other cities, and supportive local business owners and community members. He authored an aggressive Green Building Ordinance and sent it to the Planning Commission, where it was approved and sent to the City Council for a vote. Thus, the strongest green building guidelines in the county were adopted.

"[The Council members saw that the ordinance] also had other advantages for the city. Being seen as a leader in the county is good. Being seen as a leader in Northern California is good. It was also a low cost, high impact initiative for them. It was absolutely key that Bob Brown [the Community Development Director] was interested in it, and had the technical background to understand it and the broader implications. The ground was fertile for what we brought and he just took it and ran with it. He's really been a champion of sustainability issues at the City."

Kiki La Porta, Sustainable San Rafael

Build It Green (www. builditgreen.org)

The mission of this non-profit membership organization is to promote energy and resource efficient building practices in California and work with stakeholders to accelerate the adoption of green building practices.

Stop Waste (www. stopwaste.org)

This progressive county agency funded by municipal revenue is "dedicated to achieving the most environmentally sound solid waste management and resource conservation program… and promoting sustainable consumption and disposal patterns."

The agency offers public education, services and resources on waste reduction, food composting, Bay Friendly Gardening, and green building to the county's residents, business and industry, schools and local governments.

"[Our prep work] gave Bob Brown a context and a framework to build on. Our Green Building Team met with him for three or four months in a row, gratis. The City Council didn't have to form a commission and interview people and make sure they were qualified. We did all that. That's what it takes to get policy passed. Cities need to hear from experts who have done the groundwork and who can answer their questions and address their concerns."

Sue Spofford, Sustainable San Rafael

Case Study: County Policy Sheets, Sustainable Marin

Sustainable Marin is a non-profit organization that acts as the umbrella fiscal organization for all but one of the sister sustainability organizations featured in this guide. It provides organizational and fiscal support for these organizations as well as new ones coming up. Sustainable Marin also advocates and educates about sustainability at the County level.

Sustainable Marin evolved from its predecessor, "Sustainable North Bay", which in the late 1990s spurred the initiation of a county-wide plan built on a framework of long-term sustainability. It aims its efforts at tangible, measurable results and interacts constructively and aggressively with county and city officials and agencies on a variety of sustainability fronts and programs. Its board, made up almost entirely of leaders from the sister sustainability organizations, meets quarterly, and meanwhile conducts continuous networking and advocacy.

Sustainable Marin promotes policies and practices in Marin County to:

- sustain Marin County's natural capital and environmental assets,

- bolster localized economic strength and independence,

- expand locally-owned green businesses and clean-tech jobs and,

- encourage community cooperation and social justice.

Sustainable Marin sub-committees create policy sheets and do advocacy work on specific sustainability issues such as Energy, Waste, and Water. The sheets serve to educate with a general statement of the problem, philosophy of best practices, and possible actions for individuals and communities to take. They also provide members of other sustainable groups with a ready-made statement and guide for talking points should a media representative want to know their official stance.

Ideally, a policy sheet is approved in draft form by the Sustainable Marin board and then shopped around to the sister sustainability organizations in Marin County for minimal edits and buy-in. In this way, Sustainable Marin can legitimately make a statement on behalf of all the sustainability organizations in the county.

Example: Sustainable Marin's Position On Climate Disruption And Clean Energy

What is the Issue? Marin County's carbon footprint is far too high, worsening global warming.

What is happening on the issue now? Steps to reduce emissions locally are promising but tentative. Marin County and allied cities have formed Marin Clean Energy to cut carbon emissions and accelerate renewable power. Marin County has a greenhouse gas emmisions target and reduction plan. Cities are launching their own plans. Various energy efficiency initiatives have been underway, including a generic green building ordinance. Transportation authorities finally appear to be taking carbon reduction more seriously. But carbon emissions are still rising.

What Position and Steps Should Sustainable Marin Take?

Sustainable Marin endorses Community Choice Electricity Aggregation (CCA) in general and Marin Clean Energy (MCE) (via the Marin Energy Authority - MEA) in particular for their unmatched potential for reducing greenhouse gas emissions and expansion of renewable energy while keeping rates comparable to current utility suppliers. It is Sustainable Marin's intent to educate the public and decision makers about Community Choice by all appropriate means.

Sustainable Marin will consider and recommend improvements and corrections in MCE and MEA development as it progresses to emphasize maximum greenhouse gas reduction and local renewable power generation.

Sustainable Marin will voice criticism of alternative plans that don't meet MCE's goals and criteria for local renewable power and carbon footprint. A stronger portfolio of renewable power will bring greater reliability to our electricity supply, manage risk and provide a hedge against swings in natural gas prices, PG&E's continued hikes in electricity rates, volatility and, in the case of imported liquefied natural gas, dependence on imported fossil fuels.

Example: Sustainable Marin's Position On Climate Disruption And Clean Energy *(continued)*

Sustainable Marin will also support other means of reducing carbon emissions, with priority given to those means that offer the greatest potential for the least investment. Sustainable Marin supports the State's and the County's co2 reduction goals, urges expeditious adoption by city governments of effective and robust climate action plans, and views the ultimate climate protection goal, consistent with what science tells us, to be zero carbon emissions by 2050.

Sustainable Marin will take part in the "350 ppm" movement (www.350.org) to call attention to the need for more rapid emissions reductions, while recognizing that the practical possibilities for actually reducing atmospheric carbon to that level seem slim for the time being.

Sustainable Marin will support any and all means of reducing emissions from the transportation sector, reputedly the largest single source of carbon emission in Marin, giving priority to electrification of vehicles, reduction of miles traveled, revitalization of public transit, encouragement of biking and walking, and gradual evolution of town centers less dependent on vehicle travel.

Example: Sustainable Marin Policy On Zero Waste

What is the Issue?
An undiminished Marin County waste stream, high per capita throwaway rates, grossly inefficient reduction and reuse of materials.

What's Happening on the Issue Now?
Zero waste goals policies aren't being implemented, waste disposal franchise agreements lack zero waste incentives, a zero waste consultant's study has been watered down, green waste and food waste still goes to landfill, and Marin's claimed trash diversion rate is inflated.

What Position Should Sustainable Marin Take?
Sustainable Marin's policy is to promote faster and more effective implementation of the Zero Waste goals of Marin County and some cities, and to encourage cities without goals to adopt them. Sustainable Marin intends to do this by dialogue with County and city decision makers, education of the public, and robust advocacy at all levels.

Recommended Actions:
Zero Waste focuses on reducing the size of Marin's waste stream rather than continuing to process that stream through recycling. Sustainable Marin views recycling as beneficial but emphasizes instead shrinking the absolute and per capita volume of trash going to landfill and throwaway, on grounds of resource efficiency.

It is Sustainable Marin's policy to highlight and pursue those reform elements of the waste consultant's study on Zero Waste (2009) that offer the most hope of progress. Sustainable Marin views the following as having the most realistic potential impact:

Example: Sustainable Marin Policy On Zero Waste *(continued)*

- a ban on landfilling green waste and food waste
- haulers come in for rate increases and get them without question.
- a new mitigation fee on landfilling to disincentivize waste and bring Marin at least up to Bay Area levels
- composting food and green wastes in enclosed facilities while capturing energy
- a template to reform franchise agreements by including real incentives to both waste haulers and waste generators to generate and haul less waste. These agreements are "evergreen" – they never end.

Sustainable Marin should draw on what works in other jurisdictions and inform decision makers and publics about success stories in Zero Waste. Sustainable Marin supports reasonable proposals for siting local composting-energy recovery facilities in Marin, for local compost marketing and energy supply. County franchise agreements could be modified to move organic waste from being dumped to being a resource instead. Enabling language to require haulers to deliver green and food waste, for example, could be lifted from the City of Oakland's own franchise agreement.

Sustainable Marin concurs with national Sierra Club's policy on Landfill Gas to Energy (LFGTE) which calls for a stop to landfilling of materials that form more methane, and opposition to proposals for recovering legacy methane already in landfills when extraction may release more methane than is recovered for energy.

Sustainable Marin will be open to promoting effective institutional and structural reform of all waste handling matters in the County and cities. Sustainable Marin recognizes that this is a long-term proposition and politically difficult but views current barriers to Zero Waste as so dysfunctional as to require determined public exposure in order to circumvent or eliminate them. Some have been identified by past research by Marin Zero Waste Citizens' Advisory Committee (2007).

Case Study: Integrated Pest Management and Indoor Air Quality, Sustainable Novato

When Sustainable Novato's Vice President of Environmental Health Marie Chan's children were in elementary school, she and her husband began routinely receiving notices that Monsanto's herbicide Roundup would be sprayed on school athletic fields "any time between 7AM and 3PM." Because children are one of the populations most susceptible to chemical toxins, and childhood asthma can be exacerbated by volatile organics, Marie and several other parents sprang into action and began investigating.

They learned that beside the inherent problems in using pesticides at all, Roundup remains volatile for the first hour after its application. Children playing on the fields after spraying track the chemicals into their classrooms, negatively impacting indoor air quality.

Furthermore, they learned that in the late 1990s, Novato Unified School District (NUSD) had been one of the early districts in the county to craft an Integrated Pest Management (IPM) board policy limiting the use of toxins on school property. Inspiration for this policy had come from the EPA's Indoor Air Quality (IAQ) Tools for Schools program (www.epa.gov/iaq/schools), developed *"to reduce exposures*

to indoor environmental contaminants in schools through the voluntary adoption of sound indoor air quality management practices." The district's policy required maintenance crews to be trained and certified in "less-toxic" IPM techniques, and established a board IPM Committee incorporating community members to routinely review the district's IPM related activities.

In the five years or so that followed, State education budgets were chopped and many cuts were made to NUSD's budget. In the process, the IPM Committee fell by the wayside and pesticides were again used routinely on school grounds with children and teachers present.

"IPM implies you have money to fund the staff to do it." Marie Chan explains:

> *"Once a few parents got involved and after a lot of analysis, it was clear that with the best intentions the District had been trying to make budget cuts as far away from the classrooms as possible in order to educate students. We understood that, but the bottom line is to limit the potentially harmful chemicals in the environment to protect public health. We can't know how they will combine or affect different kids' bodies and sensitivities.*
>
> *In my opinion, the District had cut too deeply and the cuts had the potential to affect the health and safety of the schools'*

inhabitants. This was counter-productive to the goal of maximizing student achievement. If kids get sick, they can't learn very effectively."

Sustainable Novato arranged a meeting with the school district's CFO, its Director of Operations, Maintenance and Transportation, and members of the local non-profit Marin Beyond Pesticides Coalition (www.pesticidefreezone.org). They presented California Department of Pesticide regulations showing that while Roundup was in fact allowable under the state's IPM laws, there were very specific rules about how it and other chemicals could be used in school settings. They requested that the District adhere to these rules, as well as reinstate its IPM Policy and Committee, on which they volunteered to sit.

The CFO unilaterally declared a moratorium on spraying Roundup for the remainder of that year. He instructed the Director of Operations, Maintenance and Transportation to focus on using more benign solutions instead, and sent him to be certified in IPM through the EPA's Indoor Air Quality Tools for Schools program. This program has since been fully implemented throughout the district, and NUSD was the only district in California to receive the 2010 Achievements in Respiratory (AIR) Health

Award from the California Department of Public Health. In addition, in January 2011, NUSD was one of only five school districts in the country to win the EPA's National Excellence Award for its implementation of Tools for Schools. NUSD has achieved both the highest regional and national recognition for its accomplishments in improving indoor air quality.

NUSD's Sustainability Committee now oversees IPM and Indoor Air Quality in the district.

Sustainable Novato has had less success in its attempts to bring IPM policy to the City of Novato. Though they have provided the City Council and City Manager copies of IPM Resolutions passed by both the County and the neighboring city of San Rafael, they are one vote short of getting the support they need from the City Council to pass a city ordinance to reduce toxins in the environment.

"The City Council is overwhelmed with budget concerns and sees this as a second tier issue. Sustainable Novato is poised to move forward in our advocacy for [this] ordinance in 2012. We will give the City our support for their success. We need them to succeed."

Marie Chan, Sustainable Novato

The EPA's Indoor Air Quality Tools for Schools Program

The IAQ Tools for Schools Program is a comprehensive resource to help schools maintain a healthy environment in school buildings by identifying, correcting, and preventing IAQ problems. Poor indoor air quality can impact the comfort and health of students and staff, which, in turn, can affect concentration, attendance, and student performance. In addition, if schools fail to respond promptly to poor IAQ, students and staff are at an increased risk of short-term health problems, such as fatigue and nausea, as well as long-term problems like asthma.

Since its release in 1995, the IAQ TfS Action Kit (**www.epa.gov/iaq/schools/toolkit.html**) has been implemented in hundreds of schools across the country. Common elements of implementing the program include:

- Organizing a program with a committed group of individuals dedicated to ensuring good IAQ and with clear support from senior management
- Assessing current IAQ conditions and issues
- Creating a Plan outlining a strategic approach to identifying, resolving, and preventing IAQ problems
- Taking Actions to improve IAQ in the school that lead to increased student and staff health and productivity
- Evaluating the IAQ management program by tracking and assessing results
- Communicating the intent, results, and next steps of the IAQ management program

Case Studies: Educating Your Community

"As a 501(c)(3) non-profit, we cannot endorse candidates. On occasion board members and I have given personal endorsements, but we do it very sparingly because we don't want to burn any bridges, piss anyone off, or play favorites. We want to be friends with everybody, even if they don't think the way we think."

Pam Hartwell-Herrero, Sustainable Fairfax

Case Study: County Supervisor Election, Sustainable Mill Valley

In 2004, Southern Marin had an open seat for County Supervisor. Charles McGlashan, then a board member of Sustainable Mill Valley, decided to run. The Sustainable Mill Valley board agreed that the organization would remain neutral and avoid endorsing any particular candidate. Instead, they would work to make sure that sustainability was a focus in the race.

They developed a questionnaire for the candidates that would illuminate their accomplishments and perspectives on sustainability issues of concern to the community. Candidates were told their responses would be posted on the Sustainable Mill Valley website, published in the local newspaper and circulated on the internet to other interested community organizations. Further, Sustainable Mill Valley promised to use the winning candidate's responses as a measure of their performance in furthering sustainability in Mill Valley and Southern Marin. All of the candidates agreed to participate.

The story was picked up by the San Francisco Chronicle, and included a link to Sustainable Mill Valley's website. All of this brought a great deal of positive attention to the organization.

"I would say that was our finest moment, creating the context for the debate around sustainability. We would show up at debates and ask questions related to sustainability. We just kept bringing this topic up, and I think we really made a difference and had an important influence on the understanding and visibility of sustainability in Mill Valley."

Marie Kerpan, Sustainable Mill Valley

A tight election ensued with five people running for one seat. Charles McGlashan prevailed and won the primary, then the general election by a very narrow margin.

[Note: Tragically, Charles McGlashan passed away in March of 2011 at the age of 49, midway through his second term. He was a visionary leader of many sustainability initiatives in Marin County. His passing was a devastating loss and he is missed by many.]

Case Study: Neighborhood Canvassing, Marin Clean Energy, Sustainable San Rafael

In 2006, the State of California passed AB32, establishing a statewide greenhouse gas emissions cap and mandating every City Council in California to reduce its greenhouse gas emissions locally.

Prior to this in 2001, Rebekah Collins, co-founder of Sustainable Fairfax, led an effort among grassroots organizations to move

Example: Sustainable Mill Valley's Supervisor & City Council Candidate Sustainability Surveys

The key issues Sustainable Mill Valley wanted candidates to address were:
- Housing
- Natural Resources
- Conservation and Restoration
- Localizing the Economy
- Public Health
- Transportation
- Diversity
- Thinking Globally but Acting Locally

You can view their survey here: www.sustainablemillvalley.org/survey.html

You can also view the survey they later developed for a Mill Valley City Council election here: www.sustainablemillvalley.org/ccsurvey.html

City Councils and County Supervisors towards choosing greener, renewable energy sources that would greatly reduce greenhouse gas emissions countywide.

In 2009 a resolution that would allow municipalities to purchase power on behalf of their constituents was introduced to City Councils and the County Board of Supervisors for a vote. The resolution, to enact the Community Choice Law, would allow constituents to choose between a high percentage of renewable energy and energy generated from fossil fuel. Pacific Gas and Electric (PG&E, the sole utilities company serving the region) had been providing its customers with less than ten percent clean renewable energy and for many, this was unacceptably low.

If passed, then Marin Clean Energy (MCE) (www.marincleanenergy.info) and the Marin Energy Authority (MEA) would join to manage the change and broker the new, cleaner energy supplies. To pass, it would need a representative 'yes' vote from fifty percent of the county's population. Fairfax's Town Council was the first to sign on, and became a leader in garnering support throughout the county.

Sustainable San Rafael knew that if the resolution didn't pass it would be nearly impossible to reduce the city's greenhouse gas emissions enough to achieve the AB32 mandate. Because San Rafael had the largest population in the county, passage or failure would likely come down to how its City Council voted.

Historically, PG&E has collected billions of dollars to provide "dirty" energy in Marin County. PG&E stood to lose a substantial amount of money if the resolution were to pass, even though it would still provide the transmission infrastructure and customer service for Marin Clean Energy. Not wanting to face this potential loss, PG&E fought hard to defeat it. They hired former local politicians and their aids to attend City Council meetings and present all the reasons Marin Clean Energy was risky and destined to fail. In addition, behind the scenes, they wined and dined City Council members.

Sustainable San Rafael fought back. They spoke about it to their City Council members during open time at City Council meetings, in emails and on the street until finally they were told, *"We hear from you guys all the time. We need to hear from the people."* The City Council followed up by scheduling a series of neighborhood meetings for people to share their views.

Sustainable San Rafael partnered with the Sierra Club and Women's Energy Matters (www.womensenergymatters.org) and made a plan to canvas neighborhoods, educate people, and urge them to come to the meetings and speak up. They developed a door hanger which highlighted the top four reasons Marin Clean Energy was a good idea, and let residents know the City Council needed their permission to vote for it. In addition, they printed and distributed a stamped postcard (knowing that if it was stamped people would be more likely to send it).

The post card read:

YES, I want Marin Clean Energy. The reasons I want it are:

- It will reduce my energy bill
- It will help us disconnect from an uncertain fuel supply
- It will reduce pollution
- It will add green jobs to a green economy.

OR,

NO, I like things the way they are. I want to stay with PG&E.

Volunteers were given a script, trained, and sent out on Saturday mornings to targeted neighborhoods. Though it was not an easy task, they persisted. *"When you knock on someone's door, you've got two minutes to create a message."* said Sue Spofford of Sustainable San Rafael. *"But to get people cold to say they'll go to a meeting and speak up, or even just go to a meeting about something as dry and financial and difficult to understand [is tough]."*

They found that 100% of respondents wanted Marin Clean Energy.

Finally, the resolution came to a vote in San Rafael and passed. And though a few cities in the county initially opted not to pass it, there was enough support countywide for it to pass. The Marin Energy Authority and Marin Clean Energy have since formed and exceeded early projections for success. The remaining cities have now joined, for 100% participation county-wide.

Marin County ratepayers can now purchase "light green" (25% renewable energy) or "deep green" (100% renewable energy) from Marin Clean Energy at competitive rates. Neighboring counties are now considering this resolution and following Marin County's lead.

This success would not have been possible without the gallant efforts of the local sustainability organizations.

Case Study: Green Wednesdays, Plastic-Free Farmers Market & City-Wide Plastic Bag Ban, Sustainable Fairfax

In 2007, Sustainable Fairfax partnered with the Fairfax Farmers Market and the Inconvenient Group, a small group interested in families taking action to reduce their greenhouse gas production, to launch "Green Wednesdays." Each week at the farmers market, they celebrate the notion that every day is Earth Day and provide local residents with tips on how they can reduce their environmental footprint. Some sample tips include:

- Bring your own bags to the farmers market

- Ride your bike, use mass transit and walk

- Turn off the TV and computer in the evenings

- Get to know your neighbors

- Grow food, buy local food and pay attention to how far your food traveled to get to you

- Buy used & decomposable products

- Shop local & buy green

- Compost with worms

- Plan a 'staycation' instead of a vacation

For their inaugural event they focused on eliminating plastic bags from the farmers market. *"Some people don't think about it,"* said Pam Hartwell-Herrero, executive director of Sustainable Fairfax. *"They bring their tote bag, and then they put all their food in plastic bags and the plastic bags go into the tote bag!"*

Sustainable Fairfax purchased bio-degradable bags made of GMO-free corn to replace the plastic bags farmers normally offered. Even though the bio-bags were not a perfect alternative to plastic, they would still draw attention to the problem of rampant plastic bag use at the farmers market. Sustainable Fairfax also held a community sew-in at which 140 reusable cloth bags were made. During the inaugural event, these bags were

The Realities of Plastic

The weight of plastic produced annually in the United States is more than twice the weight of our entire population. Plastic waste is accumulating not only in our landfills, but also in our streets, parks, and waterways. A recent trawl of surface waters of the northern Pacific Ocean recovered six pounds of plastic pieces for every pound of zooplankton. If current trends of production and disposal continue, this ratio is expected to climb to 60:1 within a decade.

-from www.greensangha.org

proposed to collaborate on solutions to the plastic bag problem. While the management was open to this, and had already been working towards providing non-plastic bags for their markets, progress had been slow.

Around the same time, with the encouragement of Sustainable Fairfax and other local environmental groups, the Town of Fairfax decided to write an ordinance banning plastic bags in the city's grocery stores, shops and restaurants. Not long after publicizing their intention, plastic bag manufacturers Emerald Packaging, Inc. and Fresh Pak Corp. threatened to sue the Town, arguing that it had failed to hold an environmental impact review. The American Chemistry Council added its threat, citing that "the plastic bag ban [would] unintentionally reduce recycling and harm the environment." To avoid a lawsuit and the cost of an environmental review, the Town determined to prepare a measure for the ballot to let voters decide.

Sustainable Fairfax immediately went to work collecting the 700 signatures needed to put the measure on the ballot. To keep the issue visible in the community, they held a weekly bag exchange at the farmers market, where shoppers could bring or acquire cloth bags, bio bags, and yogurt containers for berries. They also partnered with local public radio and TV station KRCB and Good Earth Natural Foods store

handed out for free and fabric paints made available so people could personalize their bags on the spot. Event organizers gave a demonstration on avoiding plastic bag use at the market and in daily life. By the end of the evening 1,200 bio-bags had been distributed and not a single plastic bag. Being able to track that huge number of bags really hit home. But providing such large numbers of bio-bags every week wouldn't work: It was too expensive and the bags really weren't a good substitute for plastic.

Sustainable Fairfax approached the management of the Marin Farmers Markets (which oversees most of the farmers markets in the county) and to provide affordable and reusable cloth produce bags that could be sold to farmers market shoppers for just one dollar. Before Sustainable Fairfax could even finish collecting the signatures needed for the ballot measure, ninety-nine percent of the businesses in town, including its major chain grocery store, had voluntarily switched to bio-bags or paper bags. The remaining one percent were faced with the real challenge that non-plastic was not viable for them. For example, a restaurant offering soup to go couldn't use paper bags, which would break if the soup spilled, nor would bio-bags hold up against heat. Renee Goddard, one of the lead organizers and Sustainable Fairfax Board member made it her personal challenge to help each of these businesses find real solutions.

In the period leading up to Election Day, the American Chemistry Council sent every voter in town a large color flyer stating the ban would be bad for the environment, and even sent people door-to-door. The local garbage hauler countered this effort with their own pro-plastic bag ban flyer which they sent to every one of their customers in Fairfax.

On election day, just to keep things light and fun, Goddard donned a Plastic Bag Monster costume (made entirely of plastic bags) and had children and adults chase her through the downtown streets shouting, *"Get those plastic bags out of our town!"* By the closing of the polls, a whopping seventy-nine percent of Fairfax residents voted for the plastic bag ban!

The ban did not include the farmers market, however, the Market Manager was so moved by the amount of education, hard work and voter support that went into passing the ban that she worked even harder with farmers and her board to comply. The week the town-wide plastic bag ban went into effect was the week of the first market of 2009, and it was a plastic-free market.

Sustainable Fairfax and other grassroots groups have since collaborated to encourage all the municipalities in Marin County as well as County Supervisors to pass an ordinance banning plastic bags in all stores and adding fees for paper bags. A new initiative, BYO Bag Marin, (www.byobagmarin.org) planned to lead the nation in eliminating single-use bags (excluding produce and pharmacy bags). It supported a proposed county-wide ordinance that would ban merchants from offering plastic bags and place a fee on paper bags at all retail locations in Marin County.

The organization worked to garner the support of community residents and leaders, businesses and organizations to pass the ordinance and lead Marin County towards its zero waste goals.

In January 2011, the Marin County Board of Supervisors passed a Single Use Plastic Bag Ban. The ban took effect late in 2011.

Case Study: "Thinking Outside the Big Box", Sustainable Novato

In 2007, big box retailer Home Depot was poised to open a new store in the city of Novato. Sustainable Novato was concerned that this would be detrimental to Novato's small businesses, local economy and long-term community vitality.

Concerns included sales tax generated by this monster store going to out-of-state corporate headquarters rather than to the city to support community services. There would also be environmental impacts. The parcel of land Home Depot was considering was an environmentally sensitive watershed and habitat area not zoned for retail commercial use. In addition, Home Depot promoted the sale of environmentally harmful and unsustainably produced products.

Sustainable Novato joined forces with non-profits Marin Audubon, Sierra Club and

Novato Democratic Club, as well as many local small businesses to form a coalition. Together they launched the Campaign for a Healthy and Prosperous Novato: Stop Home Depot. The campaign urged community members to send letters to local papers, city government officials and the Planning Department.

It was at that time that Sustainable Novato learned about the American Independent Business Alliance (AMIBA, www.amiba. net). AMIBA offers support, information and tools to aid communities form local business alliances. AMIBA had recently done impressive and effective work promoting independent local businesses in the nearby city of Petaluma.

As luck would have it, AMIBA's co-founder and Executive Director was on a speaking tour sponsored by Cal Healthy Communities Network (www.calhcn.org). Sustainable Novato planned a community forum called *"Thinking Outside the (Big) Box, Strategies For A Strong Local Economy,"* and invited him to be their keynote speaker. Other esteemed experts would join him on a panel addressing the sub-theme: *How do the principles of sustainability apply to Novato and Home Depot?* Discussion included the following:

- A sustainable community has a thriving local economy. Home Depot is a big box that will take business away from local businesses, including paint stores, pane-glass companies, garden stores, lumber supply, and a family-owned hardware store. These businesses not only put money back into the community via sales tax dollars – they also contribute to local causes and hire local employees who in turn use their earnings to buy goods in Novato.

- A sustainable community supports its city services through a variety of sources, including sales tax revenue. Sales tax dollars from local businesses will decline significantly, with a swap of sales tax dollars earned by Home Depot versus the smaller guys.

- A sustainable community supports its local workforce. Predictably, workers from outside of Novato and Marin County will be employed due to the local cost of living and Home Depot's pay scale. This will add ever more commuters to our roads and freeways.

- A sustainable community builds structures that minimally impact the environment. A big box store drains precious energy to heat, light and cool its massive structure, and paves big parking lots to accommodate single-occupancy vehicles.

- A sustainable community cares for the natural environment and is in harmony with the biodiversity of the surrounding area. Home Depot's big-box approach to retail development is not a good fit for Novato and its environs.

Following the forum, which was well publicized and attended, Sustainable Novato and a local business put up funds to join the American Independent Business Alliance, and the Novato Independent Business Alliance was born.

"In Novato we have the Chamber of Commerce and a Downtown Business Alliance, but there's nothing that really is a voice for the local individual business owner. A lot of [what American Independent Business Alliance offers is help with] PR and marketing in terms of educating the consumer about how supporting your local business owner is good for us all as a community: There's that multiplier effect of local dollars staying local as opposed to going off to some big corporate headquarters, and of course the sales tax revenue; spending your local dollars here goes to our local sales tax coffers. And beyond that, if you spend at local individual businesses, it goes to fellow residents and workers as well."

–Annan Paterson, Sustainable Novato

Home Depot withdrew its application for the Hanna Ranch property due to public outcry, but stated it would continue to look at other properties in the area. So, while one battle was won, the fight is not over.

Case Study: Sustainability Center, Sustainable Fairfax

In May of 2000, founder Rebekah Collins had a vision for Sustainable Fairfax that included a physical space to accommodate work, community organizing and demonstration of best practices. She purchased a small, run-down single-family home across the street from the Town Hall, and with the help of many volunteers, skilled laborers and green businesses, began renovating the home to turn it into the Sustainability Center it is today. But after much initial work, the organization found it was unable to sustain itself, much less a physical site, and Rebekah had to rent out the building.

Several years later Sustainable Fairfax was reborn. Pam Hartwell-Herrero, brought in as Executive Director, won a grant to turn the neglected two thousand square foot backyard into a Permaculture demonstration site. The grant paid for a team of local Permaculture educators to lead a hands-on workshop for the community.

Over eight weekends, the workshop participants completed a demonstration garden, which included three different composting systems, rainwater harvesting, a natural building cob bench, Permaculture plantings, a water efficient drip irrigation system and Integrated Pest Management systems, with food growing throughout. The workshop created community buzz and provided a location for future classes.

The next focus was to raise money to pay the rent and re-focus work on the interior. Earlier work with county Supervisors on the Community Choice Law paid off and the County Board of Supervisors granted financial support from their discretionary funds.

Volunteers went to work and replaced some of the windows with double pane windows, installed a high efficiency toilet, replaced old light fixtures, restored the original 1920 wood floors, and installed natural linoleum in the bathroom. The claw foot bathtub was moved to the front yard for more rainwater catchment, and a do-it-yourself craft table for kids was installed. Other projects followed over time: displays on electricity generation, Marin Clean Energy, waste, water, green building, and disaster preparedness, a bookshelf for the Sustainability Library, a help desk for the volunteer staff, and retail space to address the zoning and to sell local, sustainably-made products to help pay the rent.

The Center needed staffing, so ten committed community members agreed to attend the inaugural two-day volunteer training then staff one four-hour shift per month.

The Sustainability Center opened to the public in October 2007 and has had thousands of visitors to its many classes, workshops, parties, fundraisers, and simply because it is a nice place to hang out. It has continually improved, with a growing seed library, seasonal displays of native flora and fauna, and more.

The Sustainable Backyard now has five composting systems, a Victory Garden, a cob bench and wood-fired pizza oven, and has been visited by flood prevention specialists and homeowners for its home-scale rainwater harvesting model.

[Note: After five years of operating the Sustainability Center, the board of directors decided that it was too time and energy consuming to run the center and raise funds to pay the monthly rent, and the building's owner has had to put it up for sale. Sustainable Fairfax has closed the Center's doors to the public, but continues its efforts in the community, and hopes to retain access to the Sustainable Backyard when the new owners take over.]

Case Study: Moving Toward Sustainability, Sustainable Mill Valley

In 2002, the general understanding of sustainability in Marin County was still in its infancy. In an effort to change that, Sustainable Mill Valley held a public seminar on sustainability in City Council chambers. In addition to providing education, they enrolled the participants in generating a list of visions and ideas that would make their town more sustainable. Following the seminar, they worked to develop the list into a set of clear initiatives that would address green building, climate protection, pesticide use, affordable housing and transportation. Later that Fall, they recommended the initiatives to their City Council and proposed to collaborate with the city to achieve them.

While the city of Mill Valley has yet to adopt all of the initiatives since they were proposed, it continues to make strides towards becoming more sustainable. The city's website (www.cityofmillvalley.org) indicates:

"In January 2008, the city hired a part-time Sustainability Director to provide leadership and coordination services relative to advancing sustainability related efforts in the city, and to lead the City Green committee, which determines the most effective sustainability measures to advance in the City and encourages ongoing and effective flow of communication throughout the City relative to sustainability initiatives. Some initiatives include adopting a Green Building Ordinance, joining ICLEI and the Cities for Climate Protection Campaign, adopting measures for efficient and sustainable use of resources in all city operations, and "dedicating itself to the protection of air quality, waste reduction, water and energy conservation, and the protection of wildlife and habitat."

Example: Mill Valley ~ Moving Toward Sustainability
Proposed Initiatives

1. Develop an Energy Efficiency Standards Ordinance. Under the ordinance:
- dwellings larger than 3,500 square feet would match the energy consumption of homes smaller than 3,500 square feet
- an energy efficiency worksheet would be established based on established California Title 24 energy efficiency regulations for permitting and planning commission design guidelines; the worksheet would demonstrate cost and energy savings for homeowner.
- Mill Valley Design Guidelines relating to energy conservation measures, and application of Sustainable Design Principles would be supported (e.g., "development should be efficient, ...creative in use of methods to minimize resource consumption... and use minimal energy.").

2. Pass a Resolution to join the Cities for Climate Protection campaign
- conduct a greenhouse gas inventory of the Town of Mill Valley, set targets for reduction, draft a Local Action Plan for meeting the targets, implement the plan, and monitor and report on progress.
- reap benefits in cost and environmental quality.

3. Participate in Green Building Charettes for Development of Green Building Ordinance
- Sustainable Mill Valley, City staff, developers and builders collaborate in green building seminars featuring U.S. Green Building Council and Alameda County Design Guidelines for residential development.

4. Develop a Housing Mitigation Ordinance
- Start by drafting a resolution borrowing from language available from the Marin Economic Commission (MEC) and included in the County General Plan. Look to available draft ordinance as model.

**Example: Mill Valley ~ Moving Toward Sustainability
Proposed Initiatives *(continued)***

- Establish a schedule of job types and housing needs by income class for commercial development projects. Affordable housing mitigation would be required on-site, nearby, or in the form of in-lieu fees.
- Include large homes (over 4,000 square feet), since they demand support from gardening, delivery, cleaning, and other low wage job categories.

5. Actively Reduce Pesticide Use in the Town of Mill Valley
- Sustainable Mill Valley collaborates with the Pesticide Education Group and works with the Mill Valley School District on implementation of their Integrated Pest Management (IPM) Program. Eliminate the only toxic pesticides still used in the school district on athletic fields maintained by the City.
- Adopt an Ordinance that prohibits pesticide application on all City property, requires a Least Toxic IPM Program, and includes a "noticing" ordinance requiring private property owners to submit application for pesticide use.
- Pest Management (IPM) Program. Eliminate the only toxic pesticides still used in the school district on athletic fields maintained by the City.

6. Support Sustainable Transportation in Mill Valley
- Implement a shuttle route for schools first.
- Do a feasibility study for short public shuttle route (electric cart or tram) on main artery, Miller Avenue.
- Include use of CarShare in affordable housing projects.

Case Study: Local Currency
~FairBuck, Sustainable Fairfax

The FairBuck Project began in early 2011 as a collaborative effort between volunteers from the Environmental Forum of Marin, Sustainable Fairfax, the Town of Fairfax and the Fairfax Chamber of Commerce. Their goal was to launch a three dollar trade token to promote a more vibrant local economy.

The logic behind this? Local currency encourages community members to invest in their own community, and heightens awareness of how spending locally encourages the community's economic well-being.

The FairBuck could only be spent at participating businesses in Fairfax, and community members would be encouraged to keep it circlulating by asking for it in change and spending it locally. Its use would be completely voluntary for businesses and shoppers.

In June 2011, the FairBuck Project minted its first five thousand tokens, and launched the whole idea publicly during the very popular and well-attended annual Fairfax Festival. The FairBuck project inspired the Festival poster and tee shirt design, and the FairBuck parade float won second place in the "Community" category. Volunteers enthusiastically tossed chocolate coins out

to the audience while numerous others walked around the parade and festival exchanging US dollars for FairBucks.

The FairBuck launch was featured on the cover of local newspapers, the Pacific Sun and the San Francisco Chronicle, and was covered by local radio, TV and online news sources.

With over thirty businesses participating, nearly four thousand tokens made it into circulation in the first week.

One month after the FairBuck's launch, $12,000 worth of Fairbucks were circulating around town, and $12,000 in US Dollars sat in a reserve account at First Federal Saving and Loan in case any businesses felt the need to exchange their FairBucks. Most participating businesses were finding the flow of FairBucks in and out to be equal. Fairfax shoppers were regularly requesting the FairBuck in change, often purchasing them from one business to spend at others. Parents reported using FairBucks for allowance or chore money.

After less than a year, the last of the first minting made its way out into the community, and the FairBuck Committee had designed and minted a new token for 2012. New reserve amounts were set with a portion of the reserves being based in local goods and services rather than US dollars. Beyond the reserve, additional funds will be used to mint a third batch of FairBucks. The project inspired the Fairfax town council to move its money from a large multi-national bank to a smaller local bank.

But the token is just the tip of the iceberg. As the FairBuck continues to gain attention, there are plans to grow the project to potentially include other cities in the county and possibly the entire county. There is discussion of creating a FairBuck debit card system or a scrip-based exchange for local businesses. To explore all of these options, volunteers on a Merchant Outreach Team, a Messaging Team and a Model Design Team will continue their work under the FairBuck Steering Committee.

For more information, visit:
www.fairbuck.org

Recommended Reading and Resources for Further Information

This guide is meant to get you started, but is by no means an exhaustive resource. Here is a partial list of further resources you may want to explore.

Books:

Animal Vegetable Miracle, by Barbara Kingsolver

Biomimicry: Innovation Inspired by Nature, by Janine M. Benyus

Deep Economy: The Wealth of Communities and the Durable Future, by Bill McKibben

Blessed Unrest: How the Largest Movement in the World Came into Being and Why No One Saw It Coming, by Paul Hawken

Cradle to Cradle: Remaking the Way We Make Things, by William McDonough & Michael Braungart

Creating Successful Communities, by Michael A. Mantell, et al

Designing Sustainable Communities, by Judy Corbett & Michael Corbett

Earth in Mind: On Education, Environment, and the Human Prospect, by David W. Orr

Eco-City Dimensions, edited by Mark Roseland

Eco-Economy: Building an Economy for the Earth, by Lester R. Brown & Earth Policy Institute

The Ecology of Commerce: A Declaration of Sustainability, by Paul Hawken

Facilitator's Guide to Participatory Decision-Making, by Sam Kaner

How Green is Your City? by Warren Karlenzig

How to Form a Nonprofit Corporation, by Anthony Mancuso & Nolo Press

The Key to Sustainable Cities, by Gwendolyn Hallsmith

Natural Capitalism, by Paul Hawken, Amory Lovins and Hunter Lovins

The Omnivore's Dilemma: A Natural History of Four Meals, by Michael Pollan

Our Ecological Footprint, by Mathis Wackernagel & William Rees

A Sand County Almanac (Outdoor Essays & Reflections), by Aldo Leopold

Saving Cities Saving Money, by John Hart

Silent Spring, by Rachel Carson

The Sustainability Advantage, by Bob Willard

The Sustainability Revolution: Portrait of a Paradigm Shift, by Andres R. Edwards

Sustainable Planet: Solutions for the 21st Century, edited by Betsy Taylor & Juliet Schor

Thriving Beyond Sustainability: Pathways To A Resilient Society, by Andrés R. Edwards

Tipping Point: How Little Things Can Make a Big Difference, by Malcolm Gladwell

Toward Sustainable Communities, by Mark Roseland

The Transition Handbook, From Oil Dependency to Local Resilience, by Rob Hopkins

Websites:

350.org Coalition
www.350.org

350.org is an international campaign building a movement to unite the world around solutions to the climate crisis--the solutions that science and justice demand.

Its mission is to inspire the world to rise to the challenge of the climate crisis—to create a new sense of urgency and of possibility for our planet.

American Independent Business Alliance (AMIBA)
www.amiba.net

The American Independent Business Alliance is a national 501(c)(3) non-profit organization helping communities launch and successfully operate an Independent Business Alliance® (IBA), "buy independent, buy local" campaigns, and other efforts to support community enterprise.

Ban the Bottle
www.banthebottle.net

Ban the Bottle is an organization promoting the environment by advocating bans on one-time-use plastic water bottles.

Build It Green
www.builditgreen.org

Build It Green is a non-profit membership organization whose mission is to promote healthy, energy- and resource-efficient building practices in California. They work with mainstream stakeholders in the housing industry to accelerate the adoption of green building practices. They offer trusted green building training, tools, technical expertise, and partnership opportunities for key stakeholders including public agencies, builders, developers, architects, contractors, affordable housing advocates, real estate professionals, suppliers, and homeowners.

Business Alliance for Local Living Economies (BALLE)
www.livingeconomies.org

An organization that catalyzes, strengthens and connects networks of locally owned independent businesses dedicated to building strong Local Living Economies.

Cal Healthy Communities Network (CALHCN)
www.calhcn.org

A project of the Tides Center, an independent non-profit, CALHCN is made up of organizations and individuals who share common concerns regarding poorly planned, environmentally unsustainable, economically discriminatory and socially unjust land use and development practices in California. There is also a deep commitment to social justice and economic rights for communities. The Network's goal is to advance the interests of communities in the State of California by projecting a unified voice in support of programs and policies that set new standards and raise the bar for the people of California.

Center for Non-Profit Success
www.cfnps.org

A non-profit organization whose mission is to provide the training, knowledge and resources to help non-profit organizations succeed. Provides resources, case studies, and even very inexpensive access to mentoring via a network of mentors.

The Center for Volunteer and Non-Profit Leadership of Marin
www.cvnl.org

Promotes volunteerism, strengthens non-profits, and enhances community leadership in Marin County.

Citta Slow Movement
www.cittaslowusa.org

Cittaslow is a growing network of 135 towns in 20 countries that have adopted a set of common goals and principles to preserve and enhance the quality of life for their residents and visitors. Cittaslow originated out of the concerns of four mayors for preserving the unique identities and sustainability of their small towns. It was formed in Italy in 1999, with the contribution of Carlo Petrini, founder of Slow Food.

Cittaslow Sonoma Valley (www. cittaslowsonomavalley.org) was the first community in the US to become a Cittaslow. Fairfax was approved for membership in the global and USA networks in 2010.

City of San Rafael Climate Change Action Plan

www.cityofsanrafael.org/Government/ Community_Development/Green_ Initiatives/Documents.htm

A strong example of a city's Climate Change Action Plan.

Community At Work

www.communityatwork.com

Offers consulting and training for community organizations. The organization's own Sam Kaner wrote *Facilitator's Guide to Participatory Decision-Making.*

Community Choice Aggregation

www.lgc.org/cca/docs/cca_energy_ factsheet.pdf

A law that allows communities to purchase electricity for its residents and businesses.

Earth Charter

www.un-documents.net/earth-ch

An international declaration of fundamental values and principles considered useful by its supporters for building a just, sustainable, and peaceful global society in the 21st century. The Charter *"seeks to inspire in all peoples a sense of global interdependence and shared responsibility for the well-being of the human family, the greater community of life, and future generations."*

The Earth Charter Initiative

www.earthcharterinaction.org

An extraordinarily diverse, global network of people, organizations, and institutions that participate in promoting and implementing the values and principles of the Earth Charter.

The Initiative is a broad-based, voluntary, civil society effort. Participants include leading international institutions, national governments and their agencies, university associations, non-government organizations and community-based groups, city governments, faith groups, schools and businesses – as well as thousands of individuals.

Earth House

www.earthhousecenter.org

The mission of Earth House, in Oakland, California, is to build healthy, just, and sustainable communities through education, training and multi-media communication tools. Earth House was founded in 1990 by Dr. Margaret Paloma Pavel and currently conducts local, national and international projects in a variety of print and visual media.

Environmental Forum of Marin

www.MarinEFM.org

A non-profit organization dedicated to preserving the quality of the environment through education. Provides an intensive training program and public educational services that increase understanding of ecology, environmental issues, and the planning process. Supports and advocates citizen action for the environment.

EPA's Indoor Air Quality (IAQ) Tools for Schools program

www.epa.gov/iaq/schools

The EPA developed the Indoor Air Quality (IAQ) Tools for Schools (TfS) Program to reduce exposures to indoor environmental contaminants in schools through the voluntary adoption of sound indoor air quality management practices. The IAQ Tools for Schools Program is a comprehensive resource to help schools maintain a healthy environment in school buildings by identifying, correcting, and preventing IAQ problems.

Green Sangha

www.greensangha.org

Green Sangha is dedicated to restoring our sense of oneness—healing our communities and the earth through mindful practice and awakened action. Green Sangha runs a powerful educational program on the realities of plastic in our world.

Idealist – Tools for Starting A Non-Profit

www.idealist.org/info/About/Vision

Idealist is a project of Action Without Borders, a non-profit organization founded in 1995 with offices in the United States and Argentina. Idealist is an interactive site where people and organizations can exchange resources and ideas, locate opportunities and supporters, and take steps toward building a world where all people can lead free and dignified lives.

International Council for Local Environmental Initiatives (ICLEI)

www.iclei.org

ICLEI is an international association of local governments as well as national and regional local government organizations that have made a commitment to sustainable development.

International Union for Conservation of Nature
www.iucn.org

Helps the world find pragmatic solutions to our most pressing environment and development challenges. Supports scientific research, manages field projects all over the world and brings governments, non-government organizations, United Nations agencies, companies and local communities together to develop and implement policy, laws and best practices.

Local Power, Inc.
www.localpower.com

Local Power Inc. is an Energy Service Bureau helping cities adopt, implement and manage Community Choice Aggregation (CCA) energy networks.

Marin Clean Energy
www.marincleanenergy.info

Formed by Marin County communities to provide more clean, renewable electric power at competitive rates, decrease emissions that cause global warming, and ease dependence on dirty fossil fuels. Provides consumers a choice between 25% and 100% renewable energy.

New Rules Project
Designing Rules as if Community Matters
www.newrules.org/policy-areas

A program of the Institute for Local Self-Reliance that brings fresh new policy solutions to communities and states.

Non-profit Voter Engagement Network (NVEN)
www.nonprofitvote.org

Dedicated to expanding the role of America's non-profits in voting and elections. NVEN works with state non-profit VOTE initiatives and its national website to provide resources and tools for 501(c)(3) non-profits to help their communities participate and vote.

Our Common Future - Report of the Brundtland Commission
www.worldinbalance.net/intagreements/1987-brundtland.php

This UN commissioned report first defined sustainable development and addresses the change of politics needed for achieving it.

Pesticide Free Zone
www.pesticidefreezone.org

A coalition of Marin County organizations and businesses working to change the way people view the use of pesticides. Succeeded in working with the County of Marin to reduce the use of pesticides in public spaces, implement an Integrated Pest Management (IPM) strategy and pass and IPM ordinance. Their goal today is to reduce the use of pesticides in schools and in private homes.

Plastic Bag Bans
www.plasticbaglaws.org/legislation

A resource for municipalities considering local ordinances banning the commercial us of plastic bags.

Safe Routes to School
www.saferoutesinfo.org

National program encouraging children to safely walk and bike to school.

The "Step it Up" Campaign
www.stepitup2007.org

An annual day of action dedicated to stopping climate change.

Stop Waste
www.stopwaste.org

Stopwaste.org is the Alameda County Waste Management Authority and the Alameda County Source Reduction and Recycling Board operating as one public agency dedicated to achieving the most environmentally sound solid waste management and resource conservation program for the people of Alameda County. Within this context, the Agency is committed to achieving a 75% and beyond

diversion goal and promoting sustainable consumption and disposal patterns.

Sustainability Organizations in Marin County (on whose work this guidebook is based!)
www.sustainablefairfax.org

www.sustainablemarin.org

www.sustainablemillvalley.org

www.sustainablenovato.org

www.sustainablesanrafael.org

Sustainable Mill Valley Sample Supervisor & City Council Candidate Sustainability Surveys
www.sustainablemillvalley.org/survey.html

www.sustainablemillvalley.org/ccsurvey.html

Teens Turning Green
www.teensturninggreen.org

A student led movement devoted to education and advocacy around environmentally and socially responsible choices for individuals, schools, and communities. Seeks to promote global sustainability by identifying and eliminating toxic exposures that permeate our lives, often unknowingly, yet threaten public and environmental health.

What began in the Bay Area in 2005 now has a presence at elementary, middle and high schools, universities, and student organizations across the country, as well as a strong virtual platform and media presence. The TTG chapters lead grassroots efforts that aim to raise awareness, encourage behavior change, and lobby for policy that will lessen local and global impact.

Transition US
www.transitionus.org

The Transition Movement is a vibrant, grassroots movement that seeks to build community resilience in the face of such challenges as peak oil, climate change and the economic crisis. It represents one of the most promising ways of engaging people in strengthening their communities against the effects of these challenges, resulting in a life that is more abundant, fulfilling, equitable and socially connected.

United Nations Environment Programme
www.unep.org

Program providing leadership and encouraging partnership in caring for the environment by inspiring, informing, and enabling nations and peoples to improve their quality of life without compromising that of future generations.

US Conference of Mayors Climate Protection Agreement
www.usmayors.org/climateprotection/agreement.htm

Scientific evidence and consensus continues to strengthen the idea that climate disruption is an urgent threat to the environmental and economic health of our communities. Many cities, in this country and abroad, already have strong local policies and programs in place to reduce global warming pollution, but more action is needed at the local, state, and federal levels to meet the challenge. On February 16, 2005 the Kyoto Protocol, the international agreement to address climate disruption, became law for the 141 countries that have ratified it to date. On that day, Seattle Mayor Greg Nickels launched this initiative to advance the goals of the Kyoto Protocol through leadership and action by American cities.

Women's Energy Matters
www.womensenergymatters.org

Women's Energy Matters (WEM) is a network of women and men who approach energy issues from a woman's point of view. WEM works for a rapid transition to an efficient, renewable energy system, in order to promote healthy communities and ecosystems and improve international relations. WEM also celebrates the ways women have used their own energy through the ages to work for the public good.

World Wildlife Fund for Nature
www.worldwildlife.org

An international, non-governmental organization building a future where human needs are met in harmony with nature. Its experts are active at every level – from field work to government - conserving the largest tropical rain forests, the most diverse coral reefs, and the world's most endangered species.

Online Low Cost or No-Cost Tools

Look for inexpensive or no-cost online tools such as:

Email accounts for non-profits:
www.google.com/a/help/intl/en/org/index.html

Email List Management: Constant Contact
www.constantcontact.com

Online Calendar:
www.calendarwiz.com
www.google.com

Survey tool: Survey Monkey
www.surveymonkey.com

Free or low-cost tool to create online surveys for your membership. Intelligently designed, elegant and easy to use.

Website building and hosting:
www.weebly.com

Website content management:
www.joomla.com

APPRECIATION

We would like to express deep gratitude to all those whose work and passion have inspired this guide:

Marie Chan, Pam Hartwell-Herrero, Marie Kerpan, Kiki LaPorta, Edward Mainland, Annan Paterson, John Schlag, Sue Spofford, provided the interviews around which this guide was formed. Thank you and all those who stand with you for the work you have done and continue to do for your communities and the leadership you provide to others wishing to do the same in theirs. And for always bringing new board members, new volunteers and new faces to the crowd. You never cease to inspire us.

Environmental Forum of Marin (www. marinefm.org): Thank you for providing stellar education on local ecology, environmental issues and the planning process, and for contributing so richly to building a community of well-informed citizen activists, many of whom have gone on to do tremendous work in their communities. May your programs always be full…

Andrés R. Edwards (www.andresedwards. com), sustainability consultant, educator, entrepreneur, and author of *The Sustainability Revolution* (New Society Publishers. Fifth Printing, 2005) and the newly published *Thriving Beyond Sustainability: Pathways To A Resilient Society* (New Society Publishers, 2010): Thank you for your generous and invaluable guidance and support throughout the process of compiling and writing this guide.

Scott Valentino, sevmedia in Fairfax (www.sevmedia.net): Thank you for sharing your expertise and precious time so generously to make this guide look so good!

Jen Jones: Thank you for pulling out all the stops to create the beautiful cover art and many illustrations peppering these pages.

Kristin Jakob: Thank you for your generous contribution of exquisite native grass illustrations.

Sara Shoys: Thank you for your encouragement and additional editing expertise.

Our Families: Thank you for your infinite patience, unconditional love and support of our busy-ness and passion at work in the world!

You, the Readers: Thank you for putting your passion and concern into action to better your communities and the world!

Made in the USA
Lexington, KY
24 November 2012